Leadership for School Improvement: Reflection and Renewal

A Volume in:
Leadership for School Improvement

Series Editor

Pamela S. Angelle

Leadership for School Improvement

Series Editor
Pamela S. Angelle
The University of Tennessee

Leadership for School Improvement: Reflection and Renewal (2019)
Cherie B. Gaines

Leadership for School Improvement: Reflection and Renewal

Edited by
Cherie B. Gaines

INFORMATION AGE PUBLISHING, INC.
Charlotte, NC • www.infoagepub.com

Library of Congress Cataloging-In-Publication Data

Names: Gaines, Cherie B., 1971- editor.
Title: Leadership for school improvement : reflection and renewal / edited by
  Cherie B. Gaines.
Description: Charlotte, NC : Information Age Publishing, Inc., [2019] |
  Series: Leadership for school improvement | Includes bibliographical
  references.
Identifiers: LCCN 2019002888 (print) | LCCN 2019007693 (ebook) | ISBN
  9781641136044 (Ebook) | ISBN 9781641136020 (pbk.) | ISBN 9781641136037
  (hardcover)
Subjects: LCSH: School improvement programs--United States. | Educational
  leadership--United States.
Classification: LCC LB2822.82 (ebook) | LCC LB2822.82 .L423 2019 (print) |
  DDC 371.2/07--dc23
LC record available at https://lccn.loc.gov/2019002888

Cover Art by Alexis Doss, alexisdoss.art

Copyright © 2019 Information Age Publishing Inc.

All rights reserved. No part of this publication may be reproduced, stored in a retrieval system, or transmitted, in any form or by any means, electronic, mechanical, photocopying, microfilming, recording or otherwise, without written permission from the publisher.

Printed in the United States of America

CONTENTS

Dedication viii

Introduction: Evolution of School Improvement:
Reflection and Renewal.. ix
Cherie Barnett Gaines

1. An Historical Evolution of School Improvement: 1960–2000 1
   Cherie Barnett Gaines

2. The Intersection of Federal Initiatives and School Improvement
   Policy: A Reflection on Major Federal Agendas for Education
   Reform 19
   David J. Lomascolo

3. Trends in School Improvement Research Post-NCLB 35
   Nate Koerber and Margaret M. Ritchie

4. Research Trends in School Improvement for Marginalized
   Students 53
   James A. Martinez

5. School Improvement through Shared Leadership 67
   Julia Kirk

6. Dynamic Roles of District Leaders in School Improvement and Reform 85
   Dianne F. Olivier

7. University Leadership Preparation, District Needs, and the Importance of the University Internship Supervisor in Bridging the Gap 103
   Jami Royal Berry

8. School Leadership Renewal 117
   Cherie Barnett Gaines

About the Authors 127

DEDICATION

This book is dedicated to school leaders at all levels, those who serve in formal roles as well as those who serve informally, who continuously work toward school improvement for all our children.

INTRODUCTION

EVOLUTION OF SCHOOL IMPROVEMENT

Reflection and Renewal

Cherie Barnett Gaines

INTRODUCTION

The American education system has traversed different eras of school improvement work, such as effective schools, systemic school improvement, school restructuring, school turnaround, and such. We have gone from a one-room schoolhouse with all ages of students to more specialized schools geared toward students' interests. One thing these schools seem to have in common is that the leaders are consistently seeking ways to improve the educational experience for the students. As a university instructor, I have often told my students, *You cannot make a claim just because you <u>know</u> as an educator. You must have evidence.* With that in mind, before we start this book series on Leadership for School Improvement, we need to understand, *What is School Improvement?*

The National College for Teaching and Leadership (NCTL) (n.d.) defines school improvement as the processes through which schools raise standards. This includes changes the schools make and strategies the schools use to improve student outcomes. Throughout the years, educators and policy makers have sought ways to make learning more beneficial to the students. Today, school improvement looks differently than it did between 1920 and 2000. Beginning with the Elementary and Secondary Education Act of 1965 (ESEA), researchers began to examine the impact of the schools on the achievement of students (ESEA, 1965; NCTL, n.d.). As time progressed, The American education system began to realize that other factors could also improve student achievement, such as funding, teacher quality, school climate, and leadership. Achieving sustained and continuous school improvement is not easy. In order to be impactful, one must carefully plan for school improvement with a cycle of identifying the problem, making a plan, implementing the plan, monitoring and assessing, and making adjustments.

NCTL (n.d.) suggests that the terms *school improvement* and *school effectiveness* are used interchangeably though having very different meanings. While school improvement focuses on the processes—changes made and strategies implemented—schools use to raise standards to improve student outcomes, school effectiveness concentrates on those student outcomes and characteristics of schools that affect those outcomes (NCTL, n.d.). In order for schools to improve, they must be effective. In order for schools to be effective, teachers and leaders must be equipped to perform tasks related to school improvement.

LEADERSHIP FOR SCHOOL IMPROVEMENT

Now to get to the purpose of this book: leadership for school improvement. When analyzing leaders, we must look at the traditional school leader, the principal and possibly even district and state leaders, but we must also consider other leaders in the schools, sometimes who even do not hold official leadership positions within the schools. Team or grade-level leaders, curriculum coaches, program heads, data coaches—all of these have pivotal roles in modern-day school leadership and thus provide additional opportunities for support of school improvement efforts. Leaders of highly effective schools know how to motivate, monitor, and manage their staff. Strong leaders also gain specific feedback on the performance of the school from various objective stakeholders and use that feedback to monitor and adjust processes within the school (NCTL, n.d.). In order for schools to be effective in their improvement efforts, states must support school leaders with training and resources to be successful in the development of essential school factors such as quality instruction, curriculum development, personalized learning environments for students, professional learning opportunities for educators, learning-centered leadership, links to the school community, and monitoring of progress in the schools (Murphy, 2013).

This special issue of *Leadership for School Improvement: Reflection and Renewal* presents literature that examines school improvement from a wide perspective. In the first chapter, *Evolution of School Improvement,* Cherie Gaines examines the following reports and legislation that were an impetus to school improvement: the ESEA (1965), which affirmed the nation's commitment to national educational priorities and goals; the Equality of Educational Opportunity Study, also known as the Coleman Report, which assessed the availability of equal educational opportunities to children of different race, color, religion, and national origin (Coleman, 1966); and the Jencks Report, which suggested that non-school environments are the primary force behind achievement gaps (Jencks & Brown, 1975). In *A Nation at Risk*, the National Commission on Excellence in Education identified staggering statistics of U.S. students' international educational performance and required change in 5 areas: curriculum content, standards and expectations of students, time devoted to education, teacher quality, and educational leadership and the financial support of education (Superfine, 2005; United States Department of Education, 2008). Finally, the author examines *Goals 2000*, which called for a higher standards-based curriculum and accountability measures based on those standards (Superfine, 2005). These critical elements to school improvement provide the motivation for change as discussed in following chapters in this book. Gaines approaches each from the perspective of political environments at the time, as well as the general feeling of stakeholders, identifying the increasing tension as Americans realized adding educational policies was not enough to increase academic achievement of U.S. students. Through understanding the political climate and environmental tensions at the time of these changes, the reader can follow the pathway as the United States began to exert more federal control on the education system and determine whether or not that control has, in fact, made a significant difference in school improvement.

In Chapter 2, David J. Lomascolo continues looking at policy which has centered on school improvement with the purpose of measuring and thereby increasing student achievement, focusing on policy changes to teacher accountability systems, student growth and achievement tracking, and standardized curriculums. Lomascolo examines Federal initiatives such as No Child Left Behind (NCLB) and Race to the Top, which have given way to an era of changes at the state level in teacher tenure and evaluation, as well as School Improvement Grants. The purpose of his review is to examine the intersection of policy and school improvement from 2000 to present day and draw inferences, predicated upon the literature, that serve as observations and raise questions about the implications of federal policy on education at the state level. Nate Koerber and Margaret M. Ritchie continue with Chapter 3, where they discuss research on school improvement since the approval and implementation of the NCLB and the Every Student Succeeds Act, examining the trends, patterns, and derivations that have manifested under the umbrella of school improvement. Koerber and Ritchie propose that school improvement has oscillated between an emphasis on prioritizing student outcomes and achievement via curriculum development to a focus on leadership, policy, and the procedures and processes within schools and classrooms. This chapter begins to center on identifying and developing school improvement plans that incorporate meaningful assessment and achievement initiatives within the precipice of shared leadership.

Continuing with the theme of school improvement, James A. Martinez writes Chapter 4 to examine to what degree instructional leaders serve the specific learning needs of underserved students in today's schools. Moreover, Martinez presents a discussion of literature about how much school context (e.g., urban, rural, suburban, high or low socioeconomic income, degree of ethnic diversity, percentage of English language learners, special education students) determines the degree that educational leaders succeed in addressing marginalized student needs. This chapter focuses on instructional leadership for school improvement and the degree that related educational research and policy on instructional leadership highlight the ways marginalized students are served in a variety of school configurations. Finally, connections are made which explore the manner in which these research and policy efforts align with the mission statement adopted by the American Educational Research Association's Leadership for School Improvement Special Interest Group.

The following chapters build on the strategies implemented to improve schools and examine these from the point of view of key educational contributors, examining issues from the perspectives of the principal, the district leader, and the university partner. First, Julia Kirk discusses the complex principal's role with leadership and management responsibilities and reviews the ever-changing and evolving responsibilities as state and federal mandates shift thinking in educational processes. Kirk presents literature on the principal's role in school improvement that has shifted from focus on program improvement through managerial delegation to a more comprehensive leader approach through shared leadership. Strengthening instructional practices has been shown to occur more frequently, and therefore greater increases in student achievement, when a shared leadership culture is established in a school, and this chapter reviews the principal's role in school improvement as it relates to building a culture of shared leadership.

In Chapter 6, Dianne F. Olivier examines school improvement from the viewpoint of the level of district support. Olivier suggests that as school leaders continually work toward school improvement, it is imperative to develop and maintain high levels of effective district leadership. District support directly influences the school's capacity through administrator and teacher leadership by concentrating on strategies to enhance and sustain effective teaching and learning practices. Collaborative district and school level leadership, focused on teacher empowerment, is at the heart of any scalable, sustainable school improvement effort. This chapter is directed on the roles of district personnel and the overall responsibilities at the district level regarding school reform. In addition to reviewing the critical role of district leaders with principal and teacher relationships, Olivier reviews literature about how these same relationships increases efficacy and, in turn, affects student performance within the schools.

Realizing the importance of relationship building and strong leadership for effective schools, Jami Berry examines leadership through an oft-forgotten lens, that of the university that prepares leaders for these schools and systems. Berry proposes that the importance of strong leadership preparation that includes job-embedded experiences culminating in highly qualified instructional leaders has been the focus of extensive discussion in the literature. The triangulation of alignment between this preparation, the articulated needs of the district, and the importance of the university internship supervisor in bridging the gap between the two, however, is virtually absent. This chapter builds upon existing literature to highlight the role of the university internship programmatic supervisor in providing strong support to both students and districts while simultaneously serving as an agent of continuous improvement for university preparation programs working to align content with the complex and ever-changing needs of school leaders.

The final chapter of this book presents themes found throughout the book and offers final thoughts about the trends in school improvement from the authors' perspectives. This special issue of *Leadership for School Improvement* contributes to the literature on school improvement in several ways. As educators, we must first be familiar with the politics, policies, and programs that are the impetus for school improvement as we know it today. Understanding the perceptions of school improvement from different stakeholders also provides us with the viewpoints we can use to tailor our expectations of leaders, both formal and informal, from the individual school to the university level. When we educators understand trends in education, we can gain guidance for our own professional experiences. The information in these chapters represent perspectives of educational leaders currently practicing in the field and consistently striving to build a culture of school improvement for America's educational system, hoping to begin a dialogue with other school leaders to build a system of support for all stakeholders.

REFERENCES

Coleman, J. S. (1966). *Equality of educational opportunity.* Washington, DC: United States Office of Education.

Elementary and Secondary Education Act of 1965, PL 89–10, 79 Stat. 27 (1965).

Jencks, C., & Brown, M. (1975). The effects of desegregation on student achievement: Some new evidence from the equality of educational opportunity survey. *Sociology of Education, 48*(1), 126–140.

Murphy, J. (2013). The architecture of school improvement. *Journal of Educational Administration, 51*(3), 252–263.

National College for Teaching and Leadership. (n.d.). *Theories of school improvement and effectiveness.* United Kingdom: Author.

Superfine, B. M. (2005). The politics of accountability: The rise and fall of Goals 2000. *American Journal of Education, 112*(1), 10–43.

United States Department of Education. (2008). *A nation accountable: Twenty-five years after A Nation at Risk.* Retrieved from https://www2.ed.gov/rschstat/research/pubs/accountable/accountable.pdf

CHAPTER 1

AN HISTORICAL EVOLUTION OF SCHOOL IMPROVEMENT: 1960–2000

Cherie Barnett Gaines

INTRODUCTION

Superfine (2005) suggested that while the language of the Constitution limits the federal role in education, as the nation's reach into education began to link school improvement with student achievement, political influence also began to infiltrate education statutes. As concerned citizens and legislators seek to find a balance between what is best for students and what is feasible for schools, concerns surface regarding power of state and federal government, needs of the students, and accountability. While governments strive to improve schools through mandates, lack of support and capacity to implement these policy requirements have prevented the educational systems from achieving their goals.

On May 17, 1954, *Brown v. Board of Education* ruled segregation in public schools unconstitutional (Goldstein, 2014) and set in motion a change in United States public schools for which many systems were not prepared. Shortly thereafter, on October 4, 1957, Russia launched the satellite Sputnik, and United States citizens became concerned that our own educational system was not preparing our students to be competitive in the growing science and technology needs (Goldstein, 2014). This prompted United States President Dwight D. Eisenhower to call for a reform in our education system, and with the National Defense Education Act of 1957, federal funds were directed to schools to promote innovations in education, specifically related to fields of science and foreign languages, to assure that United States students were not falling behind students in other countries (Goldstein, 2014; Superfine, 2005). Since that time, legislators, policy makers, and educators have searched for ways to improve achievement of students. Considering the sometimes futile, sometimes successful, efforts of school systems to meet the needs of students in this ever changing environment, this chapter will more closely examine the significant policies and legislation in school reform in the United States from the 1960s until 2000 and how these have impacted school improvement efforts.

CALL FOR EDUCATIONAL REFORM

In the middle of the 20th century, the United States entered a period of civil unrest fueled by segregation, discrimination, poverty, and struggle of underrepresented citizens. In 1960, United States President John F. Kennedy brought to the forefront these concerns, seeking to find a resolution to poverty. President Kennedy believed that poverty was a lifestyle rooted in culture, life choices, family life, environment, motivation, ambition, race, class, and geographic setting (Mazzuca, 2010). After Kennedy's assassination, United States President Lyndon B. Johnson carried forward initiatives began by Kennedy and declared a *War on Poverty* in the 1960s, believing that creating opportunities for those in poverty was a better solution and would lead people to self-sufficiency. As part of this initiative, the federal government created programs and instituted legislation for low income families such as the Equal Opportunities Act, addressing discrimination in employment, voting, public accommodations, and education (Bitler & Karoly, 2015; Equal Employment Opportunity Commission, n.d.); the Food Stamp Act, to strengthen the agricultural economy and to improve nutrition among low income households (Bitler & Karoly, 2015; United States Government, 2011); and the Social Security Act, a federal safety net for elderly, unemployed, and disadvantaged Americans (Bitler & Karoly, 2015; Social Security Administration, n.d.).

At the time, Congress was grounded in the idea that, based on founding principles of America and democracy, every American should have an equal opportunity for success. With the exception of the Social Security Act, the programs designed during Johnson's administration were meant to be transitory (Bitler & Karoly, 2015); however, this period began a reliance on the federal government that created short-term solutions for long-term problems (e.g., unemployment) without providing direction for permanent solutions (Goldstein, 2014; Mazzuca, 2010).

With the passage of the Civil Rights Act in 1964, federal legislators began to focus on educational rights of all children (Goldstein, 2014), though policy was loosely monitored and enforced. The limited role of the federal government in education continued through the beginning of the 21st century. As policies and legislation evolved, so did the federal government's role in education. As education in the United States lagged behind their global competitors, the role of the federal government increased, with success of students being the impetus for school improvement.

A major concern for President Kennedy, and subsequently President Johnson, was the dangerous cycle of generational poverty. Targeting youth to provide them with tools to escape poverty became a focus. Until this time, the federal government took a hands-off approach to schools and classrooms; however, President Johnson viewed education as a cure for social failure and economic inequality (Goldstein, 2014). As part of his *War on Poverty*, the needs of the United States education system became a focus, and media and educational entities called for immediate change in education, specifically focusing on how poverty impacted children in schools, with a goal of giving those entering the job market comparable skills with those throughout the country and in other countries (Bitler & Karoly, 2015; Jencks et al., 1972; Mazzuca, 2010). With the citizenry looking to the federal government for solutions to poverty, legislation was passed to advance impoverished youth, including The Child Nutrition Act, which provided funding to schools to provide nutritious lunches and eventually breakfasts to students in need (Bitler & Karoly, 2015); the Elementary and Secondary Education Act (ESEA), which funded primary and secondary education and began to emphasize standards and accountability (Bitler & Karoly, 2015; Elementary and Secondary Education Act, 1965; Paul, n.d.); and The Higher Education Act, which provided federal monies for postsecondary students (Bitler & Karoly, 2015).

PASSAGE OF ELEMENTARY AND SECONDARY EDUCATION ACT

In a one room schoolhouse in Stonewall, Texas, President Johnson signed into law the Elementary and Secondary Education Act (ESEA), which affirmed the nation's commitment to national educational priorities and goals by establishing policies based on the position that the greatest problem in low-performing schools was a lack of resources (Robelen, 2005; Standerfer, 2006). This legislation set forth funding policies for school districts, with the largest fiscal source of federal support for disadvantaged children, especially those living below the poverty line (Allison, 1966; Parker, 1994; Robelen, 2005; Wise & Rothman, 2010). The federal government supported this initiative to improve schools by providing the resources as required by ESEA. Federal funding for schools tripled between 1964 and 1966, making this the largest targeted federal investment in K–12 education (Bitler & Karoly, 2015; Robelen, 2005). Before ESEA, the government's role was limited to providing land or funding for schools and special programs but otherwise did not intrude on states' rights to make decisions on curriculum and the general operations of schools (Standerfer, 2006). As part of the ESEA statute, however, federal funds were set aside to promote school improvement for primary and secondary education. These funds were authorized for professional development of teachers, resources to support educational programs, and instructional materials to promote student learning. The passage of ESEA increased the federal role in education, specifically for students in grades PreK–12 in schools with high concentrations of children in poverty (Bitler & Karoly, 2015).

ESEA consisted of subdivisions, each focused on different areas identified as needing extra resources to improve the educational experiences of students, especially those who were considered at-risk because of their economic limitations. The forefront of ESEA was the Title I provision, which set aside billions of dollars each year to states for the education of at-risk students, especially children from low-income families (Cross, 2015; ESEA, 1965; Robelen, 2005; Superfine, 2005). The purpose of Title I was to expand and improve educational programs for vulnerable students, including preschool programs, and to close the achievement gap in reading, writing, and mathematics (Allison, 1966; Bitler & Karoly, 2015; Jeffrey, 1978). According to ESEA, Title I funds were to be to improve the educational experiences of at-risk students, which could include purchase of equipment and even funding of some school facilities, if designed to meet special educational needs of educationally deprived children (Allison, 1966; ESEA, 1965; Goldstein, 2014).

In addition to the funding policies required by ESEA, President Johnson established a National Advisory Council on the Education of Disadvantaged Children to oversee the implementation and reporting of the requirements of ESEA (ESEA, 1965; Wise & Rothman, 2010). The Council was comprised of 12 people and submitted an annual report on the progress of ESEA to the President, who would, in turn, submitted the report to Congress. After reviewing the reports and examining the impact on schools of the mandate, ESEA was to be reauthorized every five fiscal years.

Although Title I was a huge step forward in improving education for at-risk students, there were problems that emerged. Funding for Title I was federal; however, the control of these funds lay with the states, which issued the federal funds received to the local educational agencies eligible to receive the funds (ESEA, 1965). Schools were required to submit annual reports to disclose how the funds were spent; however, expenditures were loosely monitored. Additionally, at this time states had no uniform curriculum, standards, testing, or reporting; even schools in the same district often had no unitary assessment or accountability system (Standerfer, 2006; Superfine, 2005). Because of this, tracking the success of the programs and comparing the extent of student improvement from one state to the next was difficult. Perhaps most significantly, while there were detailed provisions of who was eligible to receive Title I funding, there was no requirement for states to show student learning was actually occurring (Wise & Rothman, 2010). To date, Title I provides little to no impact on student achievement (Bitler & Karoly, 2015).

ESEA also included other provisions to improve the education of at-risk students. Title II of ESEA included a program for grants for the acquisition of school library resources, textbooks, and other printed and published instructional materials in public and private elementary and secondary schools (Allison, 1966; Davenport, 2018; ESEA, 1965) and provided funding for preschools programs, while Title III provided funding for supplementary educational centers and services. Schools that served a low socioeconomic population could apply for these funds for school-based services not available in sufficient quantity or quality, such as establishing educational programs that provided a diverse range of educational experiences. Some of these programs included guidance and counseling, remedial instruction, school health, physical education, and social work services. Funds could also be used for students to gain access to advanced opportunities that would not have previously been available, such as dual enrollment programs, where students could take college-level courses and at the same time receive high school credit for those courses (ESEA, 1965).

With the passage of ESEA, policy makers assumed that improving schools by providing resources and services to at-risk students would, in turn, reduce the poverty level in the United States. The hope was that schools would receive this funding, drastically reform current practices, and reach students who had, until this point, been neglected by the educational system. President Johnson waged his *War on Poverty* and enacted ESEA but did not thoroughly question whether poverty was, in fact, solvable by education (Jeffrey, 1978; Karier, 1979). While funding for education increased, gains for the nation's poor and undereducated were modest, leaving educators and policy makers seeking additional ways to improve educational experiences for its students (Jeffrey, 1978).

THE COLEMAN REPORT

Because of the poor results from the federal intrusion of ESEA, the nation's critical view of schools continued, and the government began to question whether schools could, in fact, adequately address inequality (Downey & Condron, 2016). Following ESEA, and as a product of the Civil Rights Act of 1964, the Equality of Educational Opportunity Study (EEOS) further assessed the availability of equal educational opportunities to children of different race, color, religion, and national origin (Coleman, 1966; Goldstein, 2014; Kahlenberg, 2001; Kaviat, 2000). In the study, members of the United States Department of Health, Education, and Welfare's Office of Education investigated students and teacher quality, and the relationship between students' achievement and the schools they attended (Coleman, 1966; Kaviat, 2000). The EEOS was a longitudinal sociological study which included more than 650,000 students, 60,000 teachers, and 4,000 schools across the country and examined factors such as curriculum, facilities, textbooks, laboratories, libraries, and teacher quality (Dickinson, 2016; Downey & Condron, 2016; Jencks & Brown, 1975; Kahlenberg, 2001; Kaviat, 2000). Following the study, the committee issued the Coleman Report, so named for the committee chair, which included significant findings.

In this study, the committee first looked at the extent to which racial and ethnic groups were segregated from one another in public schools. The Coleman Report identified students from diverse backgrounds who were largely segregated from their white counterparts, as were teachers, although not as significantly as students. Second, the committee examined whether schools offered equal educational opportunities in terms of criteria of educational quality. The study uncovered significant inequalities, such as students who attended largely black schools, in learning environments with larger class sizes. Another staggering finding emanated from achievement tests. Not only were students in largely black schools learning at a lower level (Coleman, 1966; Dickinson, 2016), but nationwide, 17% of black adolescents (aged 16–17) dropped out of school as compared to only 9% of their white counterparts (Coleman, 1966). The EEOS examined teachers' quality of academic instruction in considering educational quality for children. Teachers in schools with largely minority populations typically graduated from lower quality colleges, had fewer years of teaching experience, earned smaller salaries than their counterparts in schools with a majority of white students, and had little relevant experience working with poor children of any race (Coleman, 1966; Goldstein, 2014).

Finally, the committee examined the relationship between student achievement and the types of schools attended. The Coleman Report suggested that minority students were more negatively impacted by the quality of their schools than average white students (Coleman, 1966; Goldstein, 2014). In addition to quality of the schools, peer effects had a greater influence on minority children, **recognizing that students learn vocabulary and other basic skills from each other** (Kahlenberg, 2001). While the report found schools were similar in the way they related to the achievement and socioeconomic status of their students, authors found that "the achievement of minority pupils depends more on the schools they attend than does the achievement of majority pupils" (Coleman, 1966, p. 22), suggesting that improvements in school quality made the most difference in achievement for minority children (Goldstein, 2014; Jencks & Brown, 1975).

While the original Coleman Report identified major areas of needed reform and reported study findings, the report failed to include recommendations to remedy these drawbacks (Coleman, 1966). This left states and individual school districts searching for ways to rectify these problems without any additional guidance to the already acknowledged problems. When trying to improve schools, state, district, and school leaders searched for ways to improve schools for students identified as at-risk, generally acknowledged as those from low socioeconomic families. The Coleman Report merely supported what educators knew—there were disparities—but provided no solid plan for improving the situation, which only added to the frustration of the public who continued to call for improved schools.

The Coleman Report and its implication of school quality's impact on learning for at-risk students was met with concern and out right disagreement from scholars. Researchers have questioned the findings, as well as Coleman's interpretation of the findings. Carver (1975) suggested that the data collected from EEOS show that only 10% variance of school achievement was associated with school differences compared to 90% associated with individual differences within schools. Carver (1975) also pointed out a discrepancy in the testing examined in the study, arguing that while the students' tests were reported as achievement tests, which measure current student performance, the tests were, in fact, aptitude tests, which predict future performance. Years following the initial report, researchers still argue the reported results of the EEOS. Kaviat (2000) argued that the Coleman Report suggested that student achievement was less related to the quality of schools but rather to the "social composition of the school, the student's sense of control of his environment and future, the verbal skills of teachers, and the student's family background" (para. 6). Dickinson (2016), Downey and Condron (2016), Kahlenberg (2001), and Mehta (2015) agreed and proposed that the Coleman report, when looking at the data presented, suggested that schools themselves play little role in generating or closing achievement gaps. These researchers argued that variables in academic performance were strongly linked to children's family environments but hardly at all to per pupil expenditures or other measurable school characteristics (Dickinson, 2016; Downey & Condron, 2016; Kahlenberg, 2001).

EFFECTS OF NON-SCHOOL ENVIRONMENTS

As the nation began to express more concerns about the lack of educational improvements despite increased federal funding, and as tensions continued to rise because of this, in 1970, President Nixon demanded that schools receiving Title I funds should spend money only on programs that, otherwise, could not be purchased through general funding (Davenport, 2018; Robelen, 2005). Nixon believed that providing more funding created an air of dependence on the federal government to create solutions to problems that were inherently social issues.

In 1972, Christopher Jencks and colleagues at Harvard University published a report, *Inequality: A Reassessment of the Effect of Family and School in America*, commonly referred to as The Jencks Report, and suggested that non-school environments are the primary force behind achievement gaps for at-risk students. Jencks and Brown (1975), like researchers who have come after, attempted to rebut the Coleman Report after identifying significant discrepancies with the data. Jencks and Brown (1975) reported that in the EEOS, the researchers did not control for all variables that could have explained the discrepancy in achievement of students, which may have been impacted by school resources, teacher attitudes, student motivation, or other factors (Jencks & Brown, 1975).

Jencks et al. (1972) suggested that students had access to enhanced classes and college curriculums but did recognize that resources are unequally distributed;

some have better chances to attend school with those they prefer, while some are denied access to curriculums of their choice. Jencks and Brown (1975) reported, however, that when examining data from schools, blacks and whites in the same school, especially those schools that were composed of 51%–75% white students, showed improvement. Males and females in these same schools had no significant differences in achievement; however, the researchers reported that in these schools, between first and sixth grades, blacks lost academic ground relative to white counterparts (Jencks & Brown, 1975).

Because of these issues, Jencks et al. (1972) and Jencks and Brown (1975) suggested that while the schools of at-risk students were being blamed for the inequality of student success, the researchers identified family background as having a more significant impact on cognitive skills, positing that the quality of education had very little effect on economic mobility and income (Dickinson, 2016; Downey & Condron, 2016; Jencks et al., 1972). Jencks et al. (1972) noted that poverty was not primarily hereditary while cognitive skills were; furthermore, there was no evidence that school quality could substantially reduce the extent of cognitive inequality (Jencks et al., 1972).

In the Jencks Report, researchers reported, "America spends far more money educating some children than others" (Jencks et al., 1972, p. 29). Legislators and educators focused more on students identified as at-risk because of their socioeconomic status; however, if the very wealthy or cognitively impaired were not also addressed, Jencks et al. (1972) suggested that education was not, in fact, equal for all others, regardless of economic situations. For students with any type of learning implication, researchers proposed that traditional strategies for equalizing individual earning power would not work. The researchers stated that differences between schools had minimal long-term effects—much less than effects from race, family background, and academic aptitude—so eliminating differences between schools would do almost nothing to make adults more equal (Jencks et al., 1972). Downey and Condron (2016) addressed these concerns but stressed that it was not that schools did not matter, but rather that they played a minor role in shaping achievement gaps without considering other factors. This supported Jencks et al.'s (1972) original claims that "Most differences in adult test scores are due to factors that schools do not control" (Jencks et al., 1972, p. 109).

A NATION AT RISK

Political traditions ensured that state and local education agencies would have the primary responsibilities for implementing, evaluating, and reporting educational policies and practices. As the federal role in education shifted from the hands-off approach to more direct involvement in schools, members of Congress worried the federal involvement would be an intrusion on the educational domain of states. Policy makers, however, felt that education officials, school leaders, and the American public were complacent about the state of education and called for increased attention on the nation's failing school system (United States Department of Education [USDOE], 2008). In 1983, the United States issued a clarion call for reform in *A Nation at Risk*, a report in which the National Commission on Excellence in Education identified staggering statistics of United States students' international educational performance. In this report, the Commission stated that we, as a nation, had become self-satisfied about our leading position in the world (Hewitt, 2008; Mehta, 2015; Superfine, 2005; USDOE, 2008). The Commission claimed that United States education was not shifting fast enough in a time of rapid social and economic change in the country (Superfine, 2005). The report stated that American students were behind those in other countries (Mehta, 2015; Parker, 1994), with 13% of all United States 17-year-olds and almost 40% of United States minority students being functionally illiterate (Parker, 1994; US-DOE, 1983, 2008) and 23 million American adults being functionally illiterate in everyday tasks such as reading, writing, and comprehension (USDOE, 1983).

Other risks identified by *A Nation at Risk* included the results of 19 academic tests, where American students were never first or second and, in fact, scored last seven times when compared with other industrialized nations (USDOE, 1983), confirming that the average achievement of high school students was lower than 26 years before in the United States (USDOE, 1983). Students, as a whole, were not making progress but were rather regressing in their acquired skills. Students were declining in performance on the Scholastic Aptitude Test (SAT), the test used most widely for college entrance, and were declining overall in areas such as English, higher order thinking skills, and general achievement scores (USDOE, 1983). In fact, over 50% of students who tested as gifted did not match their tested abilities with their achievement in school (USDOE, 1983), which led to an increase in remedial courses required as high school students graduated and attended colleges and universities (USDOE, 1983).

As a call to act, the Commission examined and reported on five distinct areas (Berger, 2000). In each of these areas, the Commission identified the most significant problems and called for a reform in each of the following areas: curriculum content, standards and expectations of students, time devoted to education, teacher quality, educational leadership and the financial support of education (Hewitt, 2008; USDOE, 2008). When examining the curriculum of United States schools, the Commission found that curriculum content had been "homogenized, diluted, and diffused to the point that they no longer have a central purpose" (USDOE, 1983, p. 26). Students were not being required to perform at the level previously expected of those same aged students. Being able to effectively evaluate this, however, was difficult because there were no common academic goals but rather 50 different state curricula to assess (Hewitt, 2008).

When examining standards and expectations in American schools, the Commission identified skills needed by students to be successful, such as understanding "the time, hard work, behavior, self-discipline, and motivation that are essential for high student achievement" (USDOE, 1983, p. 27). The Commission found that the amount of homework for high school seniors had decreased, with 2/3 students reporting having less than one hour of homework per night (USDOE, 1983). These same students' grades were rising while student achievement overall was declining (USDOE, 1983). In the report, the Commission recommended content standards at the national level for each core subject area and higher expectations for academic performance (Hewitt, 2008; Parker, 1994; Standerfer, 2006; US-DOE, 1983, 2008) and demanded that grades earned should be "indicators of academic achievement so they can be relied on as evidence of a student's readiness for further study" (USDOE, 1983, p. 35). States began to implement standards-based education systems with clear, grade-specific requirements (USDOE, 2008) and, based on suggestions from *A Nation at Risk*, began administering standardized tests at major transition points in education (USDOE, 1983).

In the United States, the time devoted to education was also an identified issue that correlated with the lower academic achievement of students. The Commission reported that American children spent less hours in school daily and yearly than children in other industrialized countries, such as England (Mehta, 2015; Parker, 1994; USDOE, 1983, 2008). For example, in 1983, at the time of the report, in England and other industrialized countries, high school students spent 8 hours per day, 220 days per year at school (1760 hours per year), while students in the United States spent 6 hours and 180 days (1080 hours per year), 39% less time than other in industrialized countries (USDOE, 1983). Another problem identified was *how* that time was spent in class in the United States, with life skills classes such as family living or driving counting as much toward high school credit as the time the students spent studying mathematics or science (USDOE, 1983). In the report, the Commission recommended that United States schools devise a more effective use of the school day, require students to attend a longer school day, and lengthen the school year for students (Mehta, 2015; USDOE, 1983, 2008). During this school time, teachers should devote more time to basic skills and subjects, and schools should have firm and fair codes for student conduct to reduce burden on teachers so they could focus class time on teaching (USDOE, 1983). This report also recommended states establish more stringent attendance policies to reduce absenteeism, thereby providing more time for students to learn the curriculum, and to reduce administrative burdens on the teachers to allow for actually teaching the curriculum (USDOE, 1983).

Teacher quality was another issue identified in *A Nation at Risk*, with the Commission finding that not enough academic-minded students were attracted to teaching, and of those entering the teaching field, many did not have the knowledge, skills, and training they needed to be successful and effective (USDOE, 1983, 2008). The study indicated a shortage of teachers in fields such as mathematics, science, foreign languages, and programs for gifted and talented, language minority, and handicapped students (USDOE, 1983), possibly because those with knowledge and experience in these areas could earn a larger salary in fields other than teaching. Acknowledging these problems, the Commission called for strengthening teacher preparation programs, requiring higher educational standards and more content knowledge of aspiring teachers rather than a majority of coursework focused on teaching methods (Mehta, 2015; USDOE, 1983, 2008). The Commission also recommended increasing salaries for teachers and establishing performance-based teacher compensation programs (USDOE, 1983, 2008).

A final area of focus found in *A Nation at Risk* was leadership and fiscal support of schools. The Commission was concerned that the United States was not developing the leadership necessary to administer a world-class school system (USDOE, 2008). While effective teaching was necessary, principals and superintendents also must have the "skills of persuasion, goal-setting, and developing community consensus" (USDOE, 2008, p. 7). The Commission recommended that educators and elected officials were held responsible for providing leadership necessary to achieve reforms *and* that fiscal support for the enhancements needed to bring about real change in the American educational system was provided (USDOE, 1983). While the Commission recognized that state and local officials must find a way to fund effective educational programs, recommendations were offered that the federal government help meet the needs of students such as gifted and talented, socioeconomically disadvantaged, and minority students (USDOE, 1983).

As a response to this call for continued school improvement, in the 1980s, the Effective Schools Movement (ESM) began to identify features and processes that made schools effective regardless of external factors, proposing that schools could overcome substantial challenges with effective leadership (Hallinger & Wang, 2015). Politicians had been quick to identify the problems in schools but had yet to find a solution; therefore, Americans quickly embraced this movement to find those solutions. The ESM, with a policy driven focus, began to view personal characteristics of principals as important as the contextual factors of the schools. As policy makers began to understand the gap between previous prescriptions for school reform and theory-informed, research-based practices, principals became the driving force in school improvement.

After *A Nation at Risk*, the United States education system began to see positive change. Three years after the original report, 41 states had raised high school graduation requirements, 33 states had initiated student competency tests, 30 states required teacher competency tests, 24 states embarked upon teacher career and salary enhancement programs, and SAT scores rose for American students (Parker, 1994).

Unfortunately, these initiatives were insufficient. In 2018, 35 years after *A Nation at Risk*, US schools still face struggles. In 2008, the United States Department of Education issued a followup report from the original Commission's findings and stated that while US schools have made progress, much has remained the same. Curriculum content in many schools includes simplified coursework with diluted content but with inflated course names to meet the requirements of advanced standards (USDOE, 2008). While standards have increased in curriculum areas, teaching material has not caught up with those changes, and there is often inadequate funding for schools to purchase the updated material that is available (USDOE, 2008).

CONTINUING ATTEMPTS TO IMPROVE SCHOOLS

During the last two decades of the 20th century, the federal focus on education continued to change, with the nation demanding that the government guarantee positive results from the efforts to improve schools. Along with the annual reporting, the original ESEA included a provision that the legislation had to be routinely reauthorized by the federal government. One of the most significant of these reauthorizations was the Augustus F. Hawkins-Robert T. Stafford Elementary and Secondary School Improvement Amendments of 1988 (Cross, 2015; ESEA, 1988). This reauthorization, signed by United States President Ronald Reagan, was precipitated by the concern that, after mandates which should have increased the educational achievement of at-risk students, there were not more significant academic improvements (Robelen, 2005). At-risk students, in this reauthorization, expanded to include not only those from diverse backgrounds but specifically identified children of migrant parents, indigenous children, children with disabilities, children identified as neglected, and delinquent children (ESEA, 1988).

The 1988 reauthorization of ESEA purposed to support targeted children attain grade-level proficiency and improve achievement in basic and advanced skills with focus on educational outcomes, including mandates for testing and accountability (Labor, 2017; Robelen, 2005). School administrators argued this was problematic because, particularly at the district level, there was little understanding of how to create a standards-based accountability system (Superfine, 2005). Administrators also felt that a year, the required reporting timeline, was not sufficient to show significant student growth. Additionally, the reauthorization shifted the focus of Title I to cultivating school improvement programs, requiring teachers of special at-risk students to work closely with regular classroom teachers, emphasizing advanced skills rather than basic skills for all students, while requiring increased parental involvement (Labor, 2017).

In another attempt to improve schools, on October 20, 1994, another reauthorization of ESEA, now renamed Improving America's Schools Act (IASA), took a holistic approach to examining education in America (Superfine, 2005). IASA was approved by President William J. Clinton and was designed to continue providing funds to at-risk students but also encouraged states to enact more standards-based reform for all students (Riley, 1995). Based on this version of ESEA, IASA conditioned the states' and schools' receipt of funds upon the development of standards, assessment, and accountability systems in each state (Labor, 2017; Robelen, 2005; Superfine, 2005). IASA gave schools greater access to federal funding for at-risk students, including reducing the threshold form 75% poverty to 50% poverty in order to dispense funds at a schoolwide level (Labor, 2017). IASA offered an opportunity for more local control over funding for school improvement efforts (Labor, 2017).

Additionally, IASA provided alignment between curriculum and instruction, professional development, school leadership, accountability, and school improvement, focusing on not only at-risk students but rather *all* students in the nation's schools (Riley, 1995). Professional development for teachers, administrators, and other schools staff was recognized as a significant factor in positive learning environments, recognizing that high-quality teaching is required to meet the needs of low-achieving students. (Riley, 1995). A major change that occurred with IASA was a waiver program, where schools or local districts could request funding or reporting leniency if regulatory requirements prevented the implementation of effective programs within the system (Riley, 1995). Finally, IASA required schools to seek partnerships among families, communities, and schools, recognizing the importance of stakeholder participation in a well-rounded education of students (Riley, 1995).

President Clinton signed into law *Goals 2000: Educate America Act* in 1994 which called for a higher standards-based curriculum and accountability measures based on those standards (Cross, 2015; Robelen, 2005; Superfine, 2005). Along with the initial objectives of ESEA's Title I, and the more recent reauthorization of IASA, *Goals 2000* was authorized to support the development and implementation of standards-based, systematic reform initiatives in the states (Robelen, 2005; Superfine, 2005). This legislation attempted to promote education reform on a national scale and granted the federal government more involvement in education rather than leaving it to the states to oversee, representing the greatest intrusion of the federal government into educational policy (Superfine, 2005).

On the surface, *Goals 2000* seemed to include realistic and attainable goals. The first of these was that all children in America would start school ready to learn. Additionally, all students would leave grades 4, 8, and 12 having demonstrated competency over challenging subject matter including English, mathematics, science, foreign languages, civics and government, economics, the arts, history, and geography. With this achieved, every adult in America would be literate and have the knowledge and skills necessary to compete in a global economy. In *Goals 2000*, legislators also called for a higher graduation rate, increasing to 90%, for all students (Cross, 2015). To help accomplish this, the government provided grants to help the states develop their own standards and assessment systems linked to these standards (Cross, 2015; Superfine, 2005). The grant awards allowed states an unprecedented amount of flexibility in the use of federal funds for educational purposes (Superfine, 2005).

States could choose whether or not to participate in *Goals 2000* by submitting applications to the Department of Education, explaining what would be done with grant funding from the program (Superfine, 2005). The state created improvement plan must include detailed strategies for improving teaching and learning in core content areas and would be subject to periodic review (Superfine, 2005). In addition, states must describe the process for aligning curricula, instructional materials, and assessments with state standards. States were also required to develop

Opportunity-to-Learn standards which indicated what conditions (e.g., class size, adequate supply of textbooks) had to be in place to enable students to learn effectively (Superfine, 2005). If states received funding, they were required to participate in the National Education Standards and Improvement Council (NESIC) to support systemic improvement from higher administrative level (Superfine, 2005). NESIC was composed of 19 members, appointed by the president, who reviewed national content and performance standards, the accountability arm of *Goals 2000* (Superfine, 2005).

Though full of potential, there were many problems with implementation of *Goals 2000*, especially in relation to the implementation of accountability provisions. Stephen Arons, a professor of legal studies at the University of Massachusetts, Amherst, advised that *Goals 2000* would lead to the creation of a national curriculum, and while that sounded innocuous, Arons warned that this would provoke conflict that the Department of Education would not be able to control (Superfine, 2005). While the legislation called for reform, there was a lack of capacity for the schools to implement the policy mandates, which prevented the legislation from achieving its goal (Superfine, 2005). Additionally, Superfine (2005) identified a lack of policy coherence, with conflicting or uncoordinated implementation of policy mandates between states and districts. Because of this disjointed implementation process, there was also a clear lack of accountability for noncompliance with the law (Superfine, 2005).

By the end of 1994, all states except Montana and Texas had received *Goals 2000* grants (Superfine, 2005); however, it quickly became apparent that there were many problems with this funding program. Because of the lack of federal oversight, states often did not use the funds as stated in the improvement plans (Superfine, 2005). As the NESIC began to exert more control, states began opting out, citing concerns of federal intrusion. As the states and federal government began dueling over control, the federal government began imposing sanctions on states that did not meet obligations set forth in their plans; nonetheless, the federal government continued to fund the state grants (Superfine, 2005).

Acknowledging these discrepancies, President Clinton signed into law PL 104-34, which eliminated the *Goals 2000* requirement that states had to submit school improvement plans to the Department of Education (Superfine, 2005). Along with abolishing the requirement for the improvement plan, PL 104-34 eliminated NESIC requirements from *Goals 2000* (Superfine, 2005). These changes enabled school districts in non-participating states to apply independently for *Goals 2000* funds (Superfine, 2005). This legislation further removed accountability mechanisms and increased local control over education spending, which allowed multiple states to use *Goals 2000* funding for technology implementation (Superfine, 2005) without providing justification of the need for or use of the outlay for student achievement.

As the years progressed and government oversight waned, it became obvious that *Goals 2000* had lackluster support and little effect on student achievement.

President Clinton, once the biggest supporter of the legislation, finally admitted that while *Goals 2000* started out strong, it did not live up to its promising beginning. With President Clinton's lack of support for the initiative, Congress failed to re-authorize the legislation in 1999 (Superfine, 2005).

CONCLUSION

As educational requirements of students increased, so did the requirements of schools, teachers, and administrators to provide a more effective educational experience for those students. Those responsible for educating students began to focus on improving their own education to provide a more productive learning environment. Research identified areas in which schools needed to improve, and educators and legislators sought ways to effectively employ school improvement strategies to enhance the educational experiences. The shift in focus from providing enhanced education for at-risk students to providing this experience for *all* students brought about a shift in thinking for the American education system. Educational stakeholders remained frustrated, though, with the lack of improvement and continued to ask the question: *How do we ensure quality public education for all children?* As *Goals 2000* faded and ESEA was reauthorized as No Child Left Behind, then again as Every Student Succeeds Act, the search for the elusive *one best system* continues.

REFERENCES

Allison, G. E. (1966, December). ESEA: Title I at work in Orange County, Florida. *Audiovisual Instruction*. Retrieved from http://aect.site-ym.com/?page=elementary_and_secon

Berger, J. (2000). Does top-down, standards-based reform work? A review of the status of statewide standards-based reform. *National Association of Secondary School Principals Bulletin, 84*(612), 57–64.

Bitler, M. P., & Karoly, L. A. (2015). Intended and unintended effects of the war on poverty: What research tells us and implications for policy. *Journal of Policy Analysis and Management, 34*(3), 639–696.

Carver, R. P. (1975). The Coleman Report: Using inappropriately designed achievement tests. *American Educational Research Journal, 12*(1), 77–86.

Coleman, J. S. (1966). *Equality of educational opportunity*. Washington, DC: United States Office of Education.

Cross, C. T. (2015). The shaping of federal education policy over time. *The Progress of Education Reform, 16*(2), 1–6.

Davenport, K. R. (2018). *Changes in cognitive complexity of standards: Impact on elementary school students' performance* (Order No. 10787124). Available from ProQuest Dissertations & Theses Global: The Humanities and Social Sciences Collection. (2042942177)

Dickinson, E. E. (2016, Winter). Coleman Report set the standard for the study of public education. *Johns Hopkins Magazine*. Retrieved from https://hub.jhu.edu/magazine/2016/winter/coleman-report-public-education/

Downey, D. B., & Condron, D. J. (2016). Fifty years since the Coleman Report: Rethinking the relationship between schools and inequality. *Sociology of Education, 89*(3), 207–220.

Elementary and Secondary Education Act of 1965, PL 89–10, 79 Stat. 27 (1965).

Elementary and Secondary Education Act. (1988). *Augustus F. Hawkins-Robert T. Stafford Elementary and Secondary School Improvement Amendments of 1988*, PL 100–297, 102 State. 130 (1988).

Equal Employment Opportunity Commission. (n.d.). *The law*. Retrieved from https://www.eeoc.gov/eeoc/history/35th/thelaw/index.html

Goals 2000: Educate America Act (1994). H.R. 1804. Retrieved from https://www2.ed.gov/legislation/GOALS2000/TheAct/index.html

Goldstein, D. (2014). *The teacher wars: A history of America's most embattled profession*. New York, NY: Knopf Doubleday.

Hallinger, P., & Wang, W. C. (2015). *Assessing instructional leadership with principal instructional management rating scale*. New York, NY: Springer.

Hewitt, T. W. (2008). Speculations on A Nation at Risk: Illusions and realities. *Phi Delta Kappan, 89*(8), 575–579.

Jeffrey, J. (1978). *Education for children of the poor: A study of the origins and implementation of the Elementary and Secondary Education Act of 1965*. Columbus, OH: Ohio State University Press.

Jencks, C., & Brown, M. (1975). The effects of desegregation on student achievement: Some new evidence from the equality of educational opportunity survey. *Sociology of Education, 48*(1), 126–140.

Jencks, C., Smith, M., Acland, H., Bane, M. J., Cohen, D., Gintis, H., . . . Michelson, S. (1972). *Inequality: A reassessment of the effect of family and schooling in America*. New York, NY: Basic Books.

Kahlenberg, R. D. (2001). Learning from James Coleman. *National Affairs, 35*. Retrieved from https://www.nationalaffairs.com/public_interest/detail/learning-from-james-coleman

Karier, C. J. (1979). Reviewed work: Education for children of the poor: A study of the origins and implementation of the Elementary and Secondary Education Act of 1965 by Julie Roy Jeffrey. *The American Historical Review, 84*(2), 592–593.

Kaviat, B. J. (2000, April). The social side of schooling. *Johns Hopkins Magazine*. Retrieved from http://pages.jh.edu/jhumag/0400web/18.html

Labor, C. (2017). Elementary and Secondary Education Act of 1965. *Social welfare history project*. Richmond, VA: Virginia Commonwealth University. Retrieved from https://socialwelfare.library.vcu.edu/programs/education/elementary-and-secondary-education-act-of-1965/

Mazzuca, S. (2010). The legacy of Johnson's war on poverty. *Libertarian Papers, 2*(22), 1–14.

Mehta, J. (2015). Escaping the shadow: A Nation at Risk and its far-reaching influence. *American Educator*, (Summer), 20–26.

Parker, F. (1994). *School reform, 1744–1990s, historical perspectives through key books and reports*. Washington, DC: Institution of Education Sciences.

Paul, C. A. (n.d.). *Elementary and Secondary Education Act of 1965*. Retrieved from https://socialwelfare.library.vcu.edu/programs/education/elementary-and-secondary-education-act-of-1965/

Riley, R. W. (1995). *The Improving America's Schools Act of 1994: Reauthorization of the Elementary and Secondary Education Act*. Washington, DC: US Department of Education.
Robelen, E. W. (2005). 40 years after ESEA, federal role in schools is broader than ever. *Education Week, 24*(31), 1, 42.
Social Security Administration. (n.d.). *Special collections: Chronology*. Retrieved from https://www.ssa.gov/history/1960.html
Standerfer, L. (2006). Before NCLB: The history of ESEA. *Principal Leadership, 6*(8), 2627.
Superfine, B. M. (2005). The politics of accountability: The rise and fall of Goals 2000. *American Journal of Education, 112*(1), 10–43.
United States Department of Education. (1983). *A nation at risk: The imperative for educational reform: A report to the Nation and the Secretary of Education*. United States Department of Education. Washington, DC: Author:
United States Department of Education. (2008). *A nation accountable: Twenty-five years after A Nation at Risk*. Retrieved from https://www2.ed.gov/rschstat/research/pubs/accountable/accountable.pdf
United States Government. (2011). *Enrolled acts and resolutions of Congress, 1979–2011*. Retrieved from https://catalog.archives.gov/id/299898
Wise, B., & Rothman, R. (2010). A greater society: The transformation of the federal role in education. *New Directions for Youth Development, 127*, 123–131. doi: 10.1002/yd.368

CHAPTER 2

THE INTERSECTION OF FEDERAL INITIATIVES AND SCHOOL IMPROVEMENT POLICY

A Reflection on Major Federal Agendas for Education Reform

David J. Lomascolo

INTRODUCTION

There has been (and still is) no shortage of government programs that aim to improve schools and school systems across the country. For well over a decade, with each passing administration, the United States federal government has taken an active role in trying to aid states in their efforts to improve student achievement and teacher quality. Since 2000, major government programs such as No Child Left Behind (NCLB), Race to the Top (RTTT), and School Improvement Grants (SIG) have called for educational improvements with the promise of significant funding to states for closing achievement gaps, equipping students with tools for success, and improving teacher evaluation measures. While there is little to no question about the intent of such federal programs, their effectiveness and their frequency has bolstered much debate over the extent to which the federal government should be involved in education.

Education was never an enumerated power delegated to the federal government by the U.S. Constitution and thus, decisions that influence educational reform have been largely left to the discretion of the state (Faber, 1991; Fuhrman, Goertz, & Weinbaum, 2007; Superfine, Gottlieb, & Smylie, 2012). Regardless, states have primarily adhered to federal initiatives because of the possibility of receiving federal grants. That is, if states failed to abide by provisions set forth by federal initiatives, they ran the risk of receiving little to no federal funding as well as the potential for an administrative overhaul (Johnson, 2013). For some time, decisions about how to govern policy regarding items such as teacher licensure, teacher professional development, tenure, and student achievement have been under state control (Corcoran, 2007; Fuhrman et al., 2007; Superfine et al., 2012). Similar discussions surrounding said decisions took place throughout the past eighteen years; however, with the caveat that if states did not shift and modify their policies in an efficient and timely manner, federal aid may not provide them with the monetary support needed to implement such policies in the manner by which they were intended in order to be effective (Johnson, 2013).

The purpose of this chapter is to examine literature surrounding three key federal education initiatives—NCLB, RTTT, and SIG, highlight the assumptions and weaknesses of these pieces of legislation, and offer opinions and suggestions for future research and policy enactment. Finally, I hope to generate future discussion on whether such federal initiatives have a place in state education agencies as vehicles to drive academic achievement in America's schools.

MAJOR FEDERAL EDUCATION REFORM
INITIATIVES FROM 2000–2011

The 2000 presidential election cited the U.S. educational system as one of the largest problems facing America (Gerstl-Pepin, 2002; Norris, 2001)—a sentiment that sparked public concern for the future of American student success both inside and outside of the classroom (Marschall & McKee, 2002). As an integral part of his initial campaign strategy, former President Bush pushed for more federal involvement in the country's education system with testing and accountability as the cornerstones of effective reform (Forte, 2010; Gerstl-Pepin, 2002; Hanushek, 2005). Upon election, the Bush administration wasted no time in addressing education reform as NCLB called for high-stakes testing, teacher accountability, and equality of opportunity initiatives (Hanushek, 2005; Marschall & McKee, 2002; Spring, 2006). NCLB included mandates for states to develop outcome-based standards for students to achieve proficiency in a high-stakes testing environment. Within this environment, NCLB held schools accountable for student achievement levels and issued penalties for schools that did not achieve a minimum level of annual yearly progress (AYP) (Forte, 2010; Hanushek, 2005; Johnson, 2013). As a result, NCLB began an era of educational turbulence, an effect defined as "the interplay of external variables that directly influence school reform including, primarily, the enactment of macro and micro-educational policy" (Johnson, 2013, p. 693). As a macro-policy, NCLB left the responsibility to states to develop their micro-policies for purposes of adhering to the overarching NCLB expectations and set the stage for future macro-policies such as RTTT and SIG, to do the same.

Since NCLB, research has focused on policies for improving teacher quality as a by-product of tracking and improving student achievement (Darling-Hammond & Sykes, 2003; Elliot, Isaacs, & Chugani, 2010; Finnigan, 2010; Range, Duncan, Scherz, & Haines, 2012) as federal initiatives set forth the expectation that teachers are an important leverage point for educational reform. Specifically, the American Recovery and Reinvestment Act (ARRA) urged states to place a strong emphasis on linking teacher performance to student achievement (Superfine et al., 2012).

The economic stimulus package of ARRA included $100 billion allocated to education, $7 billion of which was for RTTT and SIG (James-Burdumy & Wei, 2015). RTTT was designed to provide aid to states that agreed to implement a range of policies designed to raise student achievement. By allocating $4.35 billion in federal grants to select states to support improvements in education (Finch, 2012), the Obama administration put another macro-policy into action, leading to state enactment of teacher evaluation, tenure, and student achievement reform policies. Moreover, for states to be eligible for RTTT funds, states were required to link student growth data to teacher performance evaluations (Finch, 2012). Similarly, SIG competitively awarded grants to states with low performing schools that agreed to implement one of four prescribed intervention policies advocated by the SIG program. Both RTTT and SIG promoted related policies that placed particular emphasis on improving the quality of education in the U.S. and specifically, the nation's lowest performing schools (Dragoset et al., 2016).

From 2000–2011, federal programs were intended to manufacture comprehensive school reform (CSR) (Johnston, 2002). Slavin (2007) noted that the U.S. Department of Education defined a CSR model as one that included proper coordination of resources; effective, research-based methods and strategies; comprehensive design with aligned components; professional development; measurable goals and benchmarks; support within the school; parental and community involvement; external technical support and assistance; and evaluation strategies for student results. Further, Slavin argued a CSR model carefully takes each of those elements and integrates them with mindfulness around a "shared conception of how students will learn and develop" (Slavin, 2007, pp. 3–4). With billions of dollars put forth to improve education, it is conceivable for stakeholders to trust the federal government with following their own definition of CSR. Yet, despite well-intended, aggressive initiatives to reward states and districts with billions in funding for working to improve teacher and student performance, the federal government's role in education has faced criticism and speculation.

Of the criticisms and speculation to consider from the literature, first, researchers and the U.S. government have only just recently addressed questions regarding whether NCLB, RTTT, and SIG have been effective in fostering positive change and student growth. Second, in recent years, the development of culture and capacity within schools as a foundation for success before rapid systemic change is to take place has been noted as a necessity in order for federal initiatives to be truly successful (Fullan, 2015; Johnston, 2002). Third, federal accountability mandates have failed to provide specific funding to improve instruction, despite the argument that assurances of quality teaching, while being the most difficult facet of reform, will lead to better student outcomes (Anderson, 2002; Darling-Hammond, 2010; Desimone, 2002; Johnson, 2013; Lee & Luykx, 2005). Finally, federal reform initiatives have lacked critical elements to CSR such as research-based strategies (Adelman & Taylor, 2007), clearly defined ways to identify and evaluate schools in need of improvement (Forte, 2010), stakeholder involvement (Adelman & Taylor, 2011), and professional development for teachers (Corrigan, Higgins-D'Alessandro, & Brown, 2013; Johnson, 2013).

Federal education reform initiatives are set forth with the intent to provide a means for states to develop quality teachers and quality school programs. As a result, students are more likely to succeed on an on-going basis (Corrigan, Higgins-D'Alessandro, & Brown, 2013). While the intentions of federal initiatives are not in question here, we must question whether federal programs are accounting for all of the components necessary for efficient, systemic change to occur (Adelman & Taylor, 2007). What are the major (NCLB, RTTT, SIG) programs missing? What have they failed to take into account? Aside from the potential to receive funding, what other services and models nested within their agendas, should the federal government provide so that states may be successful? Since federal reform initiatives were meant to achieve long-standing outcomes, the ability for researchers and policy makers to objectively address these types of questions has been challenging since little longitudinal data from NCLB, RTTT, and SIG has not been available until recently (Dragoset et al., 2016; Dragoset et al., 2017; James-Burdumy & Wei, 2015; Polikoff, 2017).

For nearly twenty years, the nation has made efforts to implement CSR. Now that a significant amount of time has passed since NCLB, theoretical discussions based on school outcomes have begun to take shape so that the proficiency goals set forth by major policies can begin to be objectively assessed (Dragoset et al., 2017).

The following sections will be more discursive and speculative rather than empirical. I will discuss some of the criticisms and speculation that have resulted from assumptions underlying federal education initiatives as well as current thoughts regarding federal involvement in comprehensive education reform.

ISSUES SURROUNDING MAJOR FEDERAL EDUCATION REFORM INITIATIVES

Discussion regarding changes in education and the factors that impact reform initiatives should begin with consideration of Fullan's (2015), *The New Meaning of Educational Change*. Fullan discusses the history and meaning of educational change as well as educational change at the local, regional, and national levels. Fullan argued, "We still have not cracked the code of getting beyond the classroom door on a large scale" (p. 10). This is due, in part, to federal reform agendas failing to push for accountability, provide incentives, *and* foster capacity building. Fullan argued that if governments simply push for accountability and provide incentives, then only short-term results are achievable; however, if governments do those things in addition to fostering capacity building, effective change and continuous development are likely to occur. The need for capacity building within schools as a foundation for successful reform has existed since the inception of NCLB. According to the Center on Education Policy (2012), changing the school climate by building capacity is crucial to reform in schools with federal improvement grants, something that very few government policies have affected (Fullan, 2015).

All CSR models from NCLB, RTTT, and SIG share the common focus of "whole-system improvement" (Fullan, 2015, p. 210). Regardless, research has suggested that we should remain realistic about what such reform models can accomplish in short order (Adelman & Taylor, 2011; McGuinn, 2012); especially those that ignore the need for fully collaborative efforts at the school level (Adelman & Taylor, 2011). According to Johnston (2002), within reform agendas, the school is the primary unit of action. Johnson went on to argue that since NLCB, "few attempts have been made to explore the ability of effective teacher quality programs to achieve systemic reform" (p. 695). Thus, federal initiatives should have built-in models that help change the behaviors of individual administrators, parents, and especially teachers as a first step in building capacity for the school as a whole to systemically change (Fullan, 2015; O'Day, 2002). Federal school improvement initiatives have seemingly tinkered with rather than transformed education as they fall short of addressing barriers to learning and teaching. As a result, states have found their schools scrambling to make the necessary changes to achieve supposed rewards through funding with the aim of scholastic improvement. NCLB, RTTT, and SIG assumed that resources and supports are inherent within identified schools—a fundamental flaw, among others, of the federal reform initiatives (Adelman & Taylor, 2011; Fullan, 2010; Johnson, 2013; Waddell, 2011).

FLAWS AND ASSUMPTIONS OF NCLB, RTTT, AND SIG

No Child Left Behind

NCLB required all states to establish, by 2006, annual standardized reading and math tests, the contents of which were to be left to the states to then be assessed according to AYP benchmarks. In addition, the law mandated that by 2006, every classroom in the country must have a "qualified teacher" (Fullan, 2015, p. 206). Fullan (2015) argued that while NCLB may have started the move towards performance and progress, the law lacked a meticulous strategy for achieving lofty goals. Specifically, one flaw of NCLB was its narrow focus in causing teachers to shy away from developing general knowledge and skills within students and rather "teaching to the test" to reach AYP expectations. As a result, teachers and schools struggled to meet the unrealistic expectations of 100% proficiency in tested subjects. By failing to meet requirements of AYP, schools were quickly labeled as failures (Kolodziej, 2011) and teachers struggled to maintain morale (Byrd-Blake et al., 2010; Ladd, 2017). In their analysis of the effects of NCLB on school services and student outcomes, Reback, Rockoff, and Schwartz (2009) discovered that the pressures of NCLB led teachers to spend more time on test preparation than content exploration and caused them to feel like they had less control over the decisions made in their classrooms.

NCLB relied almost exclusively on test-based incentives without providing support for schools to assure their students were able to reach and learn at the higher standard (Reback et al., 2009). For example, NCLB outlined "high quality" teacher expectations that required teachers to possess a college degree and to have passed their state's content competency exam but did little to enforce such teacher quality provisions. By 2007, no states had met the "highly qualified teacher deadline," and 22% of states and 6% of school districts reported that they would never meet the requirements (Viteritti, 2012). In this way, NCLB may have focused on strict accountability yet fell short in fostering capacity for reform. Forte (2010) argued, "the chasm between the capacity to support identified schools and the capacity within states education agencies to provide this support all contribute to the gap between the goal and the reality" (pp. 84–85) of NCLB. Furthermore, Fullan (2015) argued, "heavy-handed accountability systems omit or seriously underestimate capacity building" (p. 206). Ladd (2017) pointed out that low achievement in schools that failed to meet AYP was more likely a reflection of the limited capacity of those schools and teachers to adequately handle the array of challenges that varying populations of children bring to the classroom, especially of those who are disadvantaged.

In retrospect, NCLB may have appeared to be comprehensive on paper, but comprehensiveness also requires coordination, and implementing NCLB's goals across an intricate network of federal and state agencies proved to be a more challenging task than was originally expected (Viteritti, 2012). By the 2007–2008 school year, schools in need of restructuring as a result of failing to meet AYP had increased by 50% from the previous year (Center on Education Policy, 2008; Forte, 2010). As the Obama administration moved into Washington, DC, the fate of American education was still quite uncertain as the intended goal of NCLB to have every child reach basic skills proficiency by 2014 had yet to be measured or achieved.

Race to the Top

RTTT dealt with many of the same issues as NCLB with a slightly different approach. While NCLB mandated schools to change, RTTT provided monetary incentives to states that reformed their education systems in specific ways. RTTT was distinct from NCLB in that it was voluntary. The philosophy behind creating a voluntary incentive program was that states would be more likely to create highly sophisticated and comprehensive ways of measuring teacher performance (Adelman & Taylor, 2013; McGuinn, 2012; Onosko, 2011; Superfine et al., 2012; Viteritti, 2012). Further, RTTT placed a greater emphasis on teacher evaluation and accountability by awarding points to states that linked student achievement and growth to teacher evaluation and retention decisions. For example, any state that disallowed the utilization of student achievement data for evaluating teachers was barred from the competition to receive RTTT funding (Viteritti, 2012). The RTTT grant moved beyond NCLB to focus on teacher effectiveness in addition to qualifications. The most distinct difference, perhaps, was that RTTT required states that received grants to adopt common K12 curriculum standards juxtaposed to NCLB, which set standards for tests but allowed states to set their own curriculum standards. This difference is noteworthy because even though NCLB developed standards for tests, it did not measure states against one another on standards or achievement. Conversely, by requiring states to adopt common K–12 standards, RTTT forced states to implement common assessments that were internationally benchmarked alongside other states that competed for and were awarded funding (Weiss, 2013).

While distinct from NCLB in several ways, RTTT was similarly flawed in its failure to account for the capacity of states to effectively compete for funding. Indeed, the competition for resources could only benefit those states with the greatest capacity to overhaul policy instead of awarding those with the greatest personnel needs and the most challenging students (Viteritti, 2012). A report by the Rand corporation (Gottfried, Stecher, Hoover, & Cross, 2011) noted that a fundamental flaw with programs such as RTTT, that encouraged states to compete for funding, was that it could increase the inequity in the distribution of resources thereby widening the gap between more and less effective state education systems. Furthermore, even states that were awarded funding through RTTT faced challenges and struggles related to capacity that went overlooked by the program (McGuinn, 2012). Fullan (2015) argued, "…the premises of RTTT are deeply flawed. If anything, hard-nosed evaluation, without any lasting capacity-building strategies, makes matters worse" (p. 207). A report by the Center on American Progress (2012) urged that realistically, states would need to build capacity for reform if they were to achieve the goals they set forth that won them funding. Specifically, states would need to invest in the personnel and technology needed to achieve desired results. The problem, however, is in the truth that many states, once awarded funding, "experienced serious strains on their resource and personnel capacity" (Weiss, 2013, p. 53). For example, states such as Tennessee and Delaware experienced staffing and resource complications. Weiss (2013) found that despite having already experienced hits to their capacity by cutting teachers and staff, each state vowed to limit hiring in the broader context of overly ambitious teacher evaluation renovations.

By using the potential for significant funding to prompt states to overhaul accountability, achievement, and personnel evaluation policies, RTTT was a macro-policy, which triggered substantial micro-policy change at the state and local levels. In so doing, RTTT appeared to "reflect genuine ambivalence about the appropriate balance between federal mandates and state discretion in education" (McGuinn, 2012, p. 140) and much like NCLB, was a catalyst for educational turbulence (Johnson, 2013). Lofty goals derived from micro-policy to appease macro-policy and initiatives can lead to detrimental outcomes for school systems and student progress if institutional capacity to support such drastic change has not been established first (Adelman & Taylor, 2011; Center for American Progress, 2012; Johnson, 2013; McGuinn, 2012; Onosko, 2011; Superfine et al., 2012; Viteritti, 2012; Weiss, 2013). Superfine et al. (2013) argued:

> RTTT does not promote strong horizontal fit across the range of important functions of the teacher workforce. Indeed, by heavily emphasizing teacher evaluation, a function that in turn directly relies on student achievement data, the RTTT further presumes that the knowledge and organizational capability to implement efficacious functions and practices already exist at state and local levels. (p. 73)

There has been no shortage of speculation surrounding RTTT. Even The Center for American Progress (2014), a usual proponent of RTTT, reported that four years after its inception, many states faced challenges meeting their goals and there was still much work to be done before any conclusive evidence of the program's intended effectiveness could be presented. As of October 2016, no significant differences existed between states that received RTTT funding and those that did not use RTTT promoted policies. In addition, there was no clear relationship, neither positive nor negative, between RTTT and student achievement (Dragoset et al., 2016).

School Improvement Grants

In addition to RTTT, another one of the Obama administration's ambitious school reform initiatives was to increase funding for SIG. SIG was specifically put forth to target the nation's worst performing schools. At the start of the 2011–2012 school year, SIG spent $3 billion in addition to its initial $546 million to aid low-income, low-performing schools (Le Floch et al., 2016; The Century Foundation, 2015). To be eligible for SIG, a school needed to be ranked in the lowest five percent in its respective state with the least recent progress in demonstrating student achievement. Schools that were eligible to receive SIG funding were then required to choose from four reform models: transformation, turnaround, restart, or close (Hurlburt, Therriault, & Le Floch, 2012; The Century Foundation 2015; Waddell, 2011). Much like NCLB and RTTT, each of the four models nested within the grant program was designed with the intent to improve student outcomes. The most popular of the four models (chosen by 74% of the first-round recipients), was transformation. In choosing transformation, schools were required to:

> (1) Replace the principal and take steps to increase teacher and school leader effectiveness; (2) institute comprehensive instructional reforms; (3) increase learning time and create community-oriented schools; and (4) provide operational flexibility and sustained support. (Center on Education Policy, 2012, p. 3)

If schools were to choose turnaround, they would still be required to replace the principal but to also evaluate all current staff and replace up to 50% of their teacher workforce. According to the Center on Education Policy (2012), in the first round of funding, over 750 schools underwent drastic overhauls of their leadership and staff.

For its initial intent, SIG seemed to be on par with NCLB and RTTT for providing monetary resources to schools in need of improvement but as Waddell (2011) argued, "The well-intended remedies mandated by the U.S. Department of Education are highly speculative, minimally effective, and overly punitive toward educational professionals" (p. 4). The SIG program has several flaws that leave it open to criticism and speculation. First, the program assumes that the low achieving schools are that way because of poor teaching and leadership from the teachers and principal. Second, there will always be schools that fall into the bottom five percent, just the same as there will always be schools that fall into the upper five percent. Simply because there will always be a bottom five percent does not mean that some schools must be failures due to their faculty. Waddell (2011) argued that it is statistically inevitable for there to be schools whose test scores rank in the bottom five percent. Third, by requiring schools that have been identified as low achieving and eligible for funding to relinquish their leadership and replace some of their teacher workforce, SIG not only assumes that the principal and teachers currently at the school are primarily responsible for the school's low achievement status, but that new principals and teachers will be easy to replace and effective agents of change.

The Center on Education Policy (2012) reported that SIG schools that opted for the transformation option in Idaho, Maryland, and Michigan found great difficulty in finding and keeping effective principals and teachers. Moreover, the prescribed transformations and turnarounds by SIG are not predicated upon any relevant, valid body of evidence to suggest such ways of instituting reform are effective (The Century Foundation, 2015; Waddell, 2011). To this end, while NCLB and RTTT failed to consider state capacity to support major reform, the SIG program overlooks school capacity to support such changes if a complete transformation is to take place. Holding schools accountable through test scores and achievement data, no matter how or in what way funding is allocated, can result in schools and states rapidly transforming their systems to appease external accountability before their own, internal accountability systems are in place (Fullan, 2015; Hargreaves & Fullan, 2012).

As of January 2017, key findings regarding the implementation and effectiveness of SIG suggest that no SIG funded model had any significant impact on student test scores, graduation, or college readiness and enrollment. Findings also suggested that in the areas of comprehensive instructional reform strategies, teacher and principal effectiveness, and operational flexibility and support, there were no differences between schools implementing a SIG model and schools that were not implementing one (Dragoset et al., 2017).

REFLECTION

There may never be a perfect solution for reforming education and getting students to perform at optimum levels 100% of the time. There also may never be a clear answer for whether the federal government should have a role in education reform. As we have seen with legislation from NCLB, RTTT, and SIG, answers, however unfavorable, come with time. Reform is a process that takes time, time that no researchers and policy makers can truly project. As long as there are states and schools with diverse populations, there will always be a need for education research that focuses on effective initiatives to drive policy for positive student outcomes. Schools will fail and schools will succeed, but the failure of schools does not necessarily mean the federal government should get involved (Hanushek, 2005), especially not by constantly proposing and enacting new measures (Hess, 1999). Johnson (2013) argued that attempts at anxiously remedying the American education system could result in teachers, students, and stakeholders living in a seemingly perpetual state of educational turbulence. This process, referred to by Hess (1999) as "policy churn," can create distraction for teachers and administrators as they get so caught up in the macro-level stipulations of the legislation, they focus solely on externals like AYP, student achievement scores, teacher evaluation measures, and applications for funding. Before schools can have the time to focus on concepts like culture and climate for building and sustaining capacity (Copland, 2003; Fullan, 2010, 2015; Weiss, 2013), schools enact micro-policies that attempt to answer the calls from macro-legislation without having done due diligence in making sure their systems are equipped for aggressive reform (Adelman & Taylor, 2011; Gottfried et al., 2011).

The past eighteen years of education in America have been observed through the lens of reform, yet there has been little statistical evidence that points to any significant improvements. What have NCLB, RTTT, and SIG missed? Could the answer simply be there is just too much reform? Johnson (2013) argued that "federally mandated accountability coupled with state-level control of standards and assessments have created a perfect storm to derail the ultimate goal of federal policy: educational reform" (p. 713). Indeed, there is a delicate balance between federal and state responsibility for school improvement (Hamann & Lane, 2004), but for that balance to be healthy, federal legislation should be structured more closely as CSR models and focus on issues of state capacity (Fullan, 2015; Gottfried et al., 2011) before projecting monetary incentives or penalties for state participation or failure. System and organization features need to be in place before a school is able to sustain continuous improvement efforts (Fullan, 2000; Hopkins, 2001). Specifically, the Sandler Foundation (2012) made recommendations for ways in which federal policy can work to aid state and school capacity for reform:

> Maintain and increase state set-asides when they are used to build comprehensive systems of support for continuous improvement and school turnaround;
>
> Create a state capacity program, a new dedicated funding stream to be used to build statewide systems of school improvement that would give districts and schools real resources, architecture, and assistance to implement school improvement efforts, including turnaround of lowest performing schools.
>
> Require reasonable matching funds to increase state-level investments in state capacity. Further, states should demonstrate maintenance of effort and that federal funds are not supplanting state investments. (p. 4)

For all their intents and purposes, NCLB, RTTT, and SIG were stimulating to our nation's educational growth. While school failure does not mean the federal government should step in, federal failure does not mean that the government should have absolutely no role in education either. The supposed "failures" of federal education reform initiatives should be considered in light of the positives that have come with those initiatives. Of course, there is research to suggest that NCLB, RTTT, and SIG were and have been generally ineffective, but there is also research to suggest that some schools and districts have benefited greatly from those programs. Before we turn over complete control of education to the federal government or dismiss their involvement entirely, research revolving around policy structure and enactment should identify weaknesses in past legislation as I have done here. From there, research stemming from the lessons learned needs to help build federal programs that are not shotgun approaches to change with billions in funding but rather, comprehensive approaches to system change. Such approaches should provide fundamentals to states and schools for building relationships, developing coherent delivery systems, and reforming the day-to-day work of students, teachers, and administrators. Change should be predicated upon empirically supported practices for dealing with potential processes and problems associated with implementing and sustaining reform initiatives; processes and problems that specifically relate to the knowledge and skills of teachers and staff, a system's ability to work collaboratively (Fullan, 2015), program coherence (Newmann, Smith, Allensworth, & Bryk, 2001), and resources such as curriculum and technology (Hopkins, 2001).

CONCLUDING THOUGHTS

Regardless of any inconclusive or negative evidence that surrounds NCLB, RTTT, and SIG, those programs nonetheless highlighted the need for something to help the nation's schools. Were the initiatives hasty or punitive? Perhaps, but focusing on assessment at some level is important because it is extremely difficult, if not impossible, to improve school performance without being able to identify areas of improvement. These programs were not perfect, but they were not wholly flawed either. As Kolodziej (2011) noted, the most important aspect of policies such as NCLB is that they drive attention towards the condition of education in its entirety. Jacobsen and Saultz (2012) found that generally, public opinion regarding who should control education suggests a balance between local, state, and federal involvement. They went on to state: "For policy decisions related to the promotion of equity across all schools, the public favors state and federal government. When issues of the day-to-day operation of schools are considered, the public believes that local officials best serve this role" (p. 388). This sentiment speaks directly to the need for capacity building at the micro-level, beginning with classroom activities to cooperation among stakeholders within the school and district before macro-level common practices and initiatives are applied across multiple jurisdictions by the federal government.

There is a time and place for federal initiatives in education. Systemic, effective change takes time. A linear relationship from the local to the federal level is necessary to begin the discourse on what effective change programs may look like and it all starts with the local foundation of capacity to support such change. It would seem, without that, we are left aware of the need for change with the absence of evidence and only the presence of speculation regarding the true effectiveness of government programs.

REFERENCES

Adelman, H. S., & Taylor, L. (2007). Systemic change for school improvement. *Journal of Educational and Psychological Consultation, 17*(1), 55–77.

Adelman, H., & Taylor, L. (2011). Turning around, transforming, and continuously improving schools: Policy proposals are still based on two- rather than a three-component blueprint. *The International Journal on School Disaffection, 8*(1), 22–34.

Anderson, R. D. (2002). Reforming science teaching: What research says about inquiry. *Journal of Science Teacher Education, 13*(1), 1–12.

Byrd-Blake, M., Afolayan, M. O., Hunt, J. W., Fabunmi, M., Pryor, B. W., & Leander, R. (2010). Morale of teachers in high poverty schools: A post-NCLB mixed methods analysis. *Education and Urban Society, 42*, 450–472.

Center for American Progress. (2012). *Race to the Top: What have we learned from the states so far? A state-by-state evaluation of Race to the Top performance.* Washington, DC: Author.

Center for American Progress. (2014). *Four years later, are Race to the Top states on track?* Washington, DC: Author.

Center on Education Policy. (2008). *A call to restructure restructuring: Lessons from the No Child Left Behind Act in five states.* Washington, DC: Scott, C.

Center on Education Policy. (2012). *Changing the school climate is the first step to reform in many schools with federal improvement grants.* Washington, DC: McMurrer, J.

Copland, M. A. (2003). Leadership of inquiry: Building and sustaining capacity for school improvement. *Educational Evaluation and Policy Analysis, 25*(4), 375–395.

Corcoran, T. B. (2007). The changing and chaotic world of teacher policy. In S. H. Fuhrman, D. K. Cohen, & F. Mosher (Eds.), *The state of educational policy research* (pp. 307–335). New York, NY: Routledge.

Corrigan, M. W., Higgins-D'Alessandro, A., & Brown, P. M. (2013). The case for adding prosocial education to current education policy: Preparing students for the tests of life, not just a life of tests. *KEDI Journal of Educational Policy, 2013*, 37–50.

Darling-Hammond, L. (2010). *The flat world and education: How America's commitment to equity will determine our future.* New York, NY: Teachers College Press.

Darling-Hammond, L., & Sykes, G. (2003). Wanted: A national teacher supply for education: The right way to meet the "highly qualified teacher" challenge. *Education Policy Analysis Archives, 11*(3), 1–55.

Desimone, L. (2002). How can comprehensive school reform models be successfully implemented? *Review of Educational Research, 72*(3), 433–479.

Dragoset, L., Thomas, J., Herrmann, M., Deke, J., James-Burdumy, S., Graczewski, C., Boyle, A., Tanenbum, C., Giffin, J., & Upton, R. (2016). *Race to the Top: Implementation and relationship to student outcomes: Executive summary* (NCEE 2017-4000) Washington, DC: National Center for Education Evaluation and Regional Assistance, Institute of Education Sciences, U.S. Department of Education.

Dragoset, L., Thomas, J., Herrmann, M., Deke, J., James-Burdumy, S., Graczewski, C., Boyle, A., Upton, R., Tanenbaum, C., Giffin, J., & Wei, T. E. (2017). *School improvement grants: Implementation and effectiveness executive summary* (NCEE 2017-4012). Washington, DC: National Center for Education Evaluation and Regional Assistance, Institute of Education Sciences, U.S. Department of Education.

Elliot, E. M., Isaacs, M. L., & Chugani, C. D. (2010). Promoting self-efficacy in early career teachers: A principal's guide for differentiated mentoring and supervision. *Florida Journal of Educational Administration and Policy, 4*(1), 131–146.

Faber, C. F. (1991). Is local control of the schools still a viable option? *Harvard Journal of Law and Public Policy, 14*(2), 447–482.

Finch, M. (2012). Precursors to policy innovation: How Tennessee entered Race to the Top. *Peabody Journal of Education, 87*(5), 576–592.

Finnigan, K. S. (2010). Principal leadership and teacher motivation under high-stakes accountability policies. *Leadership and Policy in Schools, 9*(2), 161–189.

Forte, E. (2010). Examining the assumptions underlying the NCLB federal accountability policy on school improvement. *Educational Psychologist, 45*(2), 76–88.

Fuhrman, S. H., Goertz, M. E., & Weinbaum, E. H. (2007). Educational governance in the United States: Where are we? How did we get here? Why should we care? In S. H. Fuhrman, D. K. Cohen, & F. Mosher (Eds.), *The state of education policy research* (pp. 41–61). Mahwah, NJ: Lawrence Erlbaum.

Fullan, M. (2000). The return of large scale reform. *Journal of Educational Change, 1*(1), 123.

Fullan, M. (2010). *All systems go: The change imperative for whole school reform*. Thousand Oaks, CA: Corwin and Ontario Principal's Council.

Fullan, M. (2015). *The new meaning of educational change*. New York, NY: Teachers College Press.

Gerstl-Pepin, C. (2002). Media (mis)representations of education in the 2000 presidential election. *Educational Policy, 16*(1), 37–55.

Gottfried, M. A., Stecher, B. M., Hoover, M., & Cross, A. B. (2011). *Federal and state roles and capacity for improving schools*. Santa Monica, CA: RAND Corporation.

Hamann, E. T., & Lane, B. (2004). The role of state departments of education as policy intermediaries: Two cases. *Educational Policy, 18*(3), 426–455.

Hanushek, E. A. (2005). Why the federal government should be involved in school accountability. *Journal of Policy Analysis and Management, 24*(1), 168–172.

Hargreaves, A., & Fullan, M. (2012). *Professional capital: Transforming teaching in every school*. New York, NY: Teachers College Press.

Hess, F. M. (1999). *Spinning wheels: The politics of urban school reform*. Washington, DC: The Brookings Institution.

Hopkins, D. (2001). *Differential school improvement*. New York, NY: RoutledgeFalmer.

Hurlburt, S., Therriault, S., & Le Floch, K. C. (2012). *School improvement grants: Analysis of state applications and eligible and awarded schools*. (NCEE 2012-4060). Washington, DC: U.S. Department of Education, Institute of Education Sciences, National Center for Education Evaluation and Regional Assistance.

Jacobsen, R., & Saultz, A. (2012). The polls—Trends: Who should control education? *Public Opinion Quarterly, 76*(2), 379–390.

James-Burdumy, S., & Wei, T. E. (2015). *Usage of policies and practices promoted by Race to the Top and school improvement grants: Executive summary* (NCEE 2015-4017). Washington, DC: National Center for Education Evaluation and Regional Assistance, Institute of Education Sciences, U.S. Department of Education.

Johnson, C. C. (2013). Educational turbulence: The influence of macro and micro-policy on science education reform. *Journal of Science Teacher Education, 24,* 693–715.

Johnston, B. J. (2002). Absent from school: Educational policy and comprehensive reform. *The Urban Review, 34*(3), 205–230.

Kolodziej, T. (2011). The benefits and detriments of the No Child Left Behind Act. *ESSAI, 9*(21), 59–62.

Ladd, H. F. (2017). No Child Left Behind: A deeply flawed federal policy. *Journal of Policy Analysis and Management, 36*(2), 461–469.

Lee, L., & Luykx, A. (2005). Dilemmas in scaling up innovations in elementary science instruction with nonmainstream students. *Science Education, 9*(3), 371–383.

Le Floch, K. C., O'Day, J., Birman, B., Hurlburt, S., Nayfack, M., Halloran, C., Boyle, S., Mecado-Garcia, D., Goff, R., Rosenberg, L., & Hulsey, L. (2016). *Case studies of schools receiving school improvement grants: Final report* (NCEE 2016-4002). Washington, DC: National Center for Education Evaluation and Regional Assistance, Institute of Education Sciences, U.S. Department of Education.

Marschall, M. J., & McKee, R. J. (2002). From campaign promises to presidential policy: Education reform in the 2000 election. *Educational Policy, 16*(1), 96–117.

McGuinn, P. (2012). Stimulating reform: Race to the Top, competitive grants and the Obama education agenda. *Educational Policy, 26*(1), 136–159.

Newmann, F. M., Smith, B. A., Allensworth, E., & Bryk, A. S. (2001). Instructional program coherence: What it is and why it should guide school improvement policy. *Educational Evaluation and Policy Analysis, 23*(4), 297–321.

Norris, P. (2001). US campaign 2000: Of pregnant chads, butterfly ballots and partisan vitriol. *Government and Opposition, 36*(1), 3–26.

O'Day, J. (2002). Complexity, accountability, and school improvement. *Harvard Educational Review, 72*(3), 1–37.

Onosko, J. (2011). Race to the Top leaves children and future citizens behind: The devastating effects of centralization, standardization, and high stakes accountability. *Democracy and Education, 19*(2), 1–11.

Polikoff, M. S. (2017). Is common core "working"? And where does common core research go from here? *AERA Open, 3*(1), 1–6.

Range, B. G., Duncan, H. E., Scherz, S. D., & Haines, C. A. (2012). School leaders' perceptions about incompetent teachers: Implications for supervision and evaluation. *NASSP Bulletin, 96*(4), 302–322.

Reback, R., Rockoff, J. E., & Schwartz, H. L. (2009, August). *The effects of No Child Left Behind on school services and student outcomes.* Paper presented at the NCLB: Emerging Findings Research Conference of the Urban Institute, Washington, D.C.

Sandler Foundation. (2012). *Building state capacity for school improvements: Lessons for federal policymakers.* Retrieved from: http://www.sandlerfoundation.org/wp-content/uploads/Sandler-State-Roles-Report_Lessons-for-Federal-Policymakers.pdf

Slavin, R. E. (2007). *Comprehensive school reform.* Baltimore, MD: Center for Data-Driven Reform in Education, Johns Hopkins University.

Spring, J. (2006). *American education.* New York, NY: McGraw-Hill Higher Education.

Superfine, B. M., Gottlieb, J. J., & Smylie, M. A. (2012). The expanding federal role in teacher workforce policy. *Educational Policy, 26*(1), 58–78.

The Century Foundation. (2015, July). *Lessons from school improvement grants that worked* (Issue Brief). Washington, DC: Greg Anrig.

Viteritti, J. P. (2012). The federal role in school reform: Obama's Race to the Top. *Symposium: Educational Innovation and the Law, 87*(5), 2087–2120.

Waddell, C. (2011). School improvement grants: Ransoming Title I schools in distress. *Current Issues in Education, 14*(1), 2–21.

Weiss, E. (2013). *Mismatches in the Race to the Top limit educational improvement: Lack of time, resources, and tools to address opportunity gaps puts lofty state goals out of reach.* Retrieved from http://www.epi.org/publication/race-to-the-top-goals/

CHAPTER 3

TRENDS IN SCHOOL IMPROVEMENT RESEARCH POST-NCLB

Nate Koerber and Margaret M. Ritchie

THE IMPACT OF NCLB AND ESSA

To understand the trends, movements, and concerns framing the contemporary field of education and school improvement, an examination of the evolution of U.S. education policy from the Elementary and Secondary Education Act (ESEA) of 1965 to the Every Student Succeeds Act (ESSA) of 2015 can be informative. Evaluating performance and embedding measures of accountability were required as part of the early education legislation and have continued as components of the more recent mandates (Mills, 2008). The first steps taken to address the educational needs of disadvantaged populations were addressed through ESEA's Title I. While there were few requirements to initially evaluate process or outcomes, later versions of Title I not only provided services but also set tangible outcomes for achievements and opportunities provided by funding to support high-poverty schools, giving the responsibility of managing the funds to the state and local school districts (Mills, 2008). With that responsibility, the standards and provisions set by the legislation at times have been difficult for the state and local school systems to meet (Mills, 2008).

While early educational reforms made significant strides, school improvement efforts continue to shape and develop policy that directly affects education in the United States (Edmonds, 1982). School Effectiveness Research (SER) as early as the 1970s, has played a critical role in examining factors that create "good schools" as well as how the learning "outcomes of students in both their academic and social development" (Reynolds et al., 2014, p. 197) can be positively affected. School effectiveness factors included pedagogy, the organization and structure of schools, curriculum, leadership, and educational learning environment effects within the school districts. As the challenges faced by educators and schools continued to develop, so, too, did the study of effective instruction. The scope of education and instruction came under strict scrutiny with the passage of the No Child Left Behind (NCLB) Act (2002) which mandates, specifically, that schools had to reach proficient status by the 2013–14 school year to narrow achievement gaps nationwide (Gray, Goldstein, & Thomas, 2003; Mills, 2008). As states struggled to meet the 100 percent proficiency, many states applied to the U.S. Department of Education for waivers requesting some flexibility from the law (Saultz, Fusarelli, & McEachin, 2017). States acquiring the waivers were able to develop their own intervention plans for low scoring areas, customize the accountability plan, determine how to use funds allocated for disadvantaged students, and address the individual needs of the low performing schools (House, 2014).

NCLB waivers were eventually supplanted by the 2015 ESSA which primarily transferred the responsibility of accountability, evaluation, and educational interventions to the state (Darling-Hammond et al., 2016). States were then given the responsibility to support the success of all students. Unsurprisingly, educational research began to play an even more vital role nationally, as states were now held responsible for creating their own systems of accountability and were required to "undertake different tasks—such as curriculum design, access to materials, and educator development" (Darling-Hammond et al., 2016, p. 2).

Education reform policies have historically focused on teacher performance and the essential role of teachers in the education of students; however, leadership at different levels with the educational organization has potentially a greater impact on student performance (Leithwood, Harris, & Hopkins, 2008; Louis, 2015). Local Educational Agencies (LEA) are now reevaluating their professional development and "examining teaching and learning as an organizational phenomenon" (Louis, 2015, p. 7).

As school improvement research has attempted to respond to the changing policies, mandates, and requirements for accountability since the passage of NCLB, patterns may be found in research as a reflection of policy changes. Thus, the purpose of this chapter is to investigate and identify the trends in school improvement research over the past twenty years. Following the policy influences embedded in NCLB and ESSA, a proliferation of studies focused on school effectiveness and school improvement has been generated. This chapter seeks to elucidate the most crucial factors, trends, and issues contributing to and shaping school improvement in the past two decades. Accordingly, the research question driving this chapter is: What have been the trends in school improvement research since the passage of NCLB?

METHODOLOGY

In seeking to conceptualize the trends in school improvement over the past two decades, we conducted a systematic review of empirical studies on trends in school improvement from 2000–2017. Moher et al. (2015) defined a systematic review as an attempt to "collate all relevant evidences that fits pre-specified eligibility criteria to answer a specific research question" (p. 3). Systematic reviews also entail a strict protocol because, as Moher et al. (2015) explained, a protocol, "ensures that a systematic review is carefully planned and that what is planned is explicitly documented before the review starts, thus promoting consistent conduct by the review team, accountability, research integrity, and transparency of the eventual completed review" (p. 1). Therefore, the protocol for this chapter necessitated a strict structure to maintain reliability and consistency throughout. Our protocol plan was as follows:

1. Accredited and reputable online educational databases (ERIC, Academic Search Complete) were selected for full-text searches of *school improvement trends, trends in school improvement,* and *school improvement movements.*
2. Peer-reviewed articles, books, and book chapters discovered via the database searches were then catalogued on a research matrix and categorized by author, publication date, article title, methodology, and whether studies were conducted on a local or national level.
3. The matrix was then expanded with a findings section where relevant conclusions and outcomes were listed from each article and chapter utilizing the authors' words.
4. The literature was then coded employing in vivo and descriptive coding (Saldana, 2013) to identify key words from each article and book chapter. These key words emerged as the categories of factors and trends mentioned most frequently. Thus, key words and categories became the foundation of our findings.

In total, over 125 articles, books, and book chapters were reviewed; however, this number was significantly reduced in the matrix, as articles largely deviating from a central focus on school improvement were removed to maintain validity. The research matrix consisted of 73 articles, books, and book chapters. Of those 73, 37 were local studies and 36 were national studies. The methodologies included case studies, comparative analysis, literature analysis, interviews, surveys, and localized assessment data; 44 of these were qualitative studies, 17 were quantitative studies, and 12 implemented a mixed-method approach.

Initially, the review was organized and divided chronologically, by year span, in the following way—prior to 2000, 2000–2005, 2006–2010, and 2010–present; however, some additional articles outside this timeframe were reviewed retroactively due to frequency of reference so that a broader, more extensive picture of trends in school improvement would be painted. The findings were later iteratively and heuristically coded to categorize emerging themes within the literature (Saldana, 2013). The first cycle of coding was strictly in vivo to prioritize the author's own words; the second cycle focused on descriptive coding which was conducive to identifying themes across the literature (Saldana, 2013). These descriptive codes and key words were then compared across the different time arrangements and synonymous terms were amalgamated. From this process, several areas of focus emerged in regard to trends in school improvement, namely—collaborative leadership and shared leadership (17 references), distributed leadership (15 references), school improvement planning and data practices (12 references), leadership development and leadership behaviors (12 references) and cultures of learning and learning communities (11 references). Due to reference frequency within the research, these five themes were highlighted as critical to school improvement and will be discussed at length in our findings.

FINDINGS

Collaborative Leadership and Shared Leadership

In an effort to address the many initiatives associated with school improvement, as well as move away from top-down leadership, principals began to change the leadership structure by cultivating leadership within the school. The principals' base of influence moved to one of "professional expertise and moral imperative rather than line authority" (Murphy, 2015, p. 17). Hallinger and Heck's (2010) findings supported the idea that collaborative leadership leads to more sustainable school improvement than the singular principal led school. This trend did away with teachers who taught in isolation, relying on educational coursework and experiential memories to guide their teaching. Collaborative leadership made use of governance structures and processes that empowered staff and students, encouraged broad participation in decision making, and fostered shared accountability for student learning (Hallinger & Heck, 2010). Teachers began to take a more active role in the curriculum and professional development. Collaborative leadership allowed the schools to focus on the inclusion of a broader range of leaders within the school environment and with those that directly impacted teaching and learning (Hallinger & Heck, 2010). Moreover, studies articulated a link between collaboration and student outcomes. Goddard, Goddard, and Tschannen-Moran's (2007) quantitative study of students and teachers in a Midwestern school district found that teacher collaboration had a positive impact on student achievement.

Goddard et al.'s (2007) research showed a "strong relationship between teacher collaboration for instructional improvement and student achievement" (p. 879) reinforcing the notion that teacher collaboration does, in fact, improve schools.

As school structures changed to operate with teams and collaboration, teachers learned that guidance related to their own teaching and learning was found in the experiences of their colleagues. Teachers become more open to suggestions and critique of their peers and found support for change to improve their teaching style (Fairman & Mackenzie, 2015). As relationships developed, a level of trust that had not existed before was established between teachers (Fairman & Mackenzie, 2015). New teachers valued the expertise of veteran teachers and the experienced teachers appreciated the new approaches to instruction and curriculum brought to the discussion by novice teachers (Fairman & Mackenzie, 2015). Teachers felt that it was safe to share ideas and ask questions and the "reciprocity in these relationships allowed both novice and veteran teachers to feel rewarded" (Fairman & Mackenzie, 2015, p. 78). Fairman and Mackenzie (2015) found that there was a shift in the perspective of teachers from concern for the students in their own classroom to a greater concern improving learning for the student body as a whole.

Clearly, one of the challenges of collaborative leadership is the ability of the principal to relinquish control. When the principal's power or authority is changed in any way, the principal risks vulnerability, resulting in some principals' balking at embracing collaborative leadership (Harris, 2004). Nonetheless, while the extent to which principals accept collaborative practices can vary, depending on the context. Furthermore, a relationship between the principal and teachers who support collaborative leadership tend to improve schools and demonstrate better performance (Marks, 2013).

Distributed Leadership

Distributed leadership was originally used as a lens to study patterns of leadership across the organization and to describe the exchanges between organizational context and organization personnel (Bennett & Harvey, 2003; Bolkan & Holmgren, 2012; Kelly & Saunders, 2010; Spillane, Halverson, & Diamond, 2001). More recently, distributed leadership has become a term to describe the "'leadership that is shared within, between and across organizations,' (Harris, 2013a, p. 12)" (Harris & DeFlaminis, 2016, p. 141). School leaders who practice distributed leadership encourage the involvement of teachers by assigning specific leadership responsibilities.

The collective body of principals and teachers who are able to pool their expertise can have a significant impact on school improvement and the opportunity for effective professional development (Harris, 2004). When teachers are empowered to lead in areas that have significance and importance to their own interests, a greater commitment to the performance of students develops, and in turn, student outcomes demonstrate improvement (Harris, 2004).

Sigurðardóttir and Sigþórsson's (2016) study of leadership capacity and how it evolved through school improvement found that a change in the structure of leadership could impact school improvement. Over the course of a ten-year period, the principal in Sigurðardóttir and Sigþórsson's research changed his leadership style from one of authority that included a small group of teachers to a more widespread form of leadership that involved many teachers in leadership function. The new roles provided opportunities for teachers to influence and be involved in the decisions regarding the functioning of the school. The principal required that certain methods and structure be maintained and observed but the delegated leadership allowed for creativity, boosted enthusiasm and resulted in "an ownership of the improvement efforts" (Sigurðardóttir & Sigþórsson, 2016, p. 600).

Distributed leadership, like collaborative leadership, requires that principals are willing to delegate their leadership responsibilities to others. Principals may not trust their faculty to assume such responsibilities. Principals may also feel vulnerable in their authority to their parent constituencies and in their support in the transfer of leadership (Harris, 2004). Furthermore, teachers may resist assuming leadership roles and may feel that their time is limited with responsibilities to classroom teaching already maximized. Other potential barriers include concerns of hierarchy established among teachers that could create an atmosphere that fosters less congeniality and increases the possibility of risk or conflict. Teachers also may question how the leadership is distributed, concerned that teacher leadership not become an extension of the principal's agenda (Fairman & Mackenzie, 2015; Harris, 2004; Lambert, 2003). Overcoming these challenges requires a committed principal, teacher-leaders with strong interpersonal skills, and a school climate that encourages change and supports leadership from teachers (Harris, 2004). Given the right conditions, distributed leadership can have a positive impact on teacher efficacy, student performance, and school improvement (Bennett & Harvey, 2003; Fairman & Mackenzie, 2015; Harris, 2004).

School Improvement Planning and Data Practices

A significant impact of NCLB and ESSA legislation was that schools were held responsible for creating school improvement plans as a strategic outline to attain proficiency status and address areas of deficiency. School improvement plans require accountability measures and the means by which to evaluate, assess, and monitor student learning and growth (Darling-Hammond et al., 2016; Mills, 2008). As a result, this prioritized and generated research that focused on creating efficacious school improvement plans and data practices to evaluate and support those plans (DuFour, 2004; Fairman & Mackenzie, 2012; Heck & Hallinger, 2010; Johnson & Sillman, 2012; O'Day, 2002). Edmonds (1982) recognized the need for "evaluative materials that permit assessment" (p. 18) nearly twenty years before the approval of NCLB and its accountability stipulations. This need for evaluative materials was now mandated, as schools sought the means by which to statistically evaluate growth.

Concurrently, school improvement plans became the blueprint for building school improvement and strategically addressing accountability (DuFour, 2004; Heck & Hallinger, 2010; Hopkins, 2001; Johnson & Sillman, 2012). The plans were intended to link to school improvement, creating a sense of school community and an environment where a shared school mission, leadership development, collaboration, data analysis, educational initiatives, and strategies can be shared and discussed openly (DuFour, 2004; Fairman & Mackenzie, 2012; Heck & Hallinger, 2010; Hopkins, 2001; Johnson & Sillman, 2012; O'Day, 2002).

While shared, cooperatively constructed school improvement plans became the outline for data analysis, building capacity, and generating school gains, the research also highlighted that these plans were not static artifacts; rather, these plans were consistently and constantly reinvented in light of the data and shifting school dynamics (DuFour, 2004; Fairman & Mackenzie, 2015; Heck & Hallinger, 2010; Johnson & Sillman, 2012). This continual redevelopment of school improvement plans and initiatives were how "education began its struggle to recast itself as consistent with the political, social, and economic DNA of an information society" (Murphy, 2015, p. 1079). Across the literature, school improvement plans were connected to positive school growth when they were designed as a consistently developing shared mission, so that new data and new information would constantly influence decisions and instruction (DuFour, 2004; Fairman & Mackenzie, 2012; Heck & Hallinger, 2010; Johnson & Sillman, 2012; Murphy, 2015; O'Day, 2002).

Leadership Development and Leadership Behavior

Across the literature, leadership was referenced in some capacity in nearly every article, chapter, and study. The majority of the research investigated and emphasized distributed leadership, collaborative leadership, and shared/teacher leadership; however, ample research also prioritized the role and influence of the leader. Within this context, the capacity and development of targeted leadership styles and behaviors, at an administrative level, through preparation and evaluation were also described as paramount to school improvement (Dimmock, 2012; Hassenpflug, 2013; Hauge, Norenes, & Vedøy, 2014; Heck & Hallinger, 2010; Hopkins, 2001; Hughes & Kritsonis, 2006; Jean-Marie, Normore, & Brooks, 2009; Johnson & Sillman, 2012; Kaniuka, 2012; Leithwood, 2016; Leithwood, Louis, Anderson, & Wahlstrom, 2009; Robinson, Lloyd, & Rowe, 2008). This section will elucidate on the literature that intertwined leadership styles and behaviors, leadership capacity, leadership preparation and development, and leadership evaluation with school improvement (Dimmock, 2012; Hassenpflug, 2013; Hauge et al., 2014; Heck & Hallinger, 2010; Hopkins, 2001; Hughes & Kritsonis, 2006; Jean-Marie et al., 2009; Johnson & Sillman, 2012; Kaniuka, 2012; Leithwood, 2016; Leithwood et al., 2009; Murphy, 2015; Robinson et al., 2008).

Across the literature, the role of administrative leadership was investigated through the behaviors and styles of the leaders, the preparation and evaluations systems in place in reference to leadership, and the influence of leadership behaviors on teachers, teacher capacity, and school communities (Fairman & Mackenzie, 2012; Hassenpflug, 2013; Hughes & Kritsonis, 2006; Johnson & Sillman, 2012; Kaniuka, 2012; Robinson et al., 2008). This research analyzed the factors and behaviors of leadership that led to school improvement and findings repeatedly emphasized behaviors associated with instructional leadership (Kaniuka, 2012). Hassenpflug (2013) describes the behaviors and influence of such leaders in the following way:

> the principal has to be seen as a credible instructional leader by teachers in order for meaningful dialogues about student achievement to occur at the school. Principals have to be able to demonstrate confidence rather than apologize for lacking knowledge or engage in disingenuous pretense. Teachers have to be able to respect a principal as an instructional leader, and that leadership has to be authentic. (p. 91)

Hassenpflug (2013) and Murphy (2015) argued that once leaders demonstrated instructional leadership behaviors, essentially mastery of content and pedagogical initiatives, then teachers' instructional practices develop and, therefore, effective student learning is cultivated. Robinson et al. (2008) reinforced this notion by saying:

> The leadership dimension that is most strongly associated with positive student outcomes is that of promoting and participating in teacher learning and development. Because the agenda for teacher professional learning is endless, goal setting should play an important part in determining the teacher learning agenda. Leaders' involvement in teacher learning provides them with a deep understanding of the conditions required to enable staff to make and sustain the changes required for improved outcomes. It is the responsibility of leaders at all levels of the system to create those conditions. (p. 667)

Again, those leadership behaviors that nurture teacher capacity are directly aligned with progressive student growth and school improvement. These leadership behaviors are intentional, empowering, and catered to their staff. Robinson et al. (2008) goes on to say that, "Educational leadership involves not only building collegial teams, a loyal and cohesive staff, and sharing an inspirational vision. It also involves focusing such relationships on some very specific pedagogical work" (p. 665). Thus, school improvement is tied directly with a leader's ability to identify and utilize specific educational initiatives to best serve teachers' and students' needs. Kaniuka (2012) reported similar conclusions and stressed the role leader behaviors play in cultivating teacher capacity, by bringing about "effective change not only in student performance but commensurate changes in teacher capacity" (p. 343). Research which examined a high school transitioning from one effective principal to another highlighted specific behaviors that may be *passed down* to the new principal (Johnson & Sillman, 2012). One area prioritized in the findings was the principal's ability to develop people and their capacity as educators. The principal facilitated teacher development, seen as an essential skill that promoted the growth and improvement of the high school (Johnson & Sillman, 2012). While the abilities and behaviors of a leader to influence instruction, teacher capacity, and student outcomes are reiterated across the literature of school improvement, this concept also evokes a plethora of considerations.

Hopkins (2001), Robinson et al. (2008), Hughes and Kritsonis (2006), and Hassenpflug (2013) all acknowledge the necessity of further research in teacher development as well as the influence context plays on leadership behaviors and leadership development. Hopkins (2001) considered the role of context as so influential that he differentiated specific leadership behaviors based upon the contextual factors of schools. Hopkins (2001) divided schools into failing or ineffective schools, low achieving schools, and good or effective schools to highlight leadership behaviors and strategies, deemed most effective according to the school context. Robinson et al. (2008) echoed similar considerations noting that "Schools at different stages of development will need different leadership emphases" (p. 668). Hassenpflug (2013) reiterated the influence of context in the hiring of new principals, emphasizing that schools should seek out leaders who specialize in their specific deficit areas.

Across the literature, researchers recognized the need for further research in leadership development and leadership behaviors. Robinson et al. (2008) summarized this concern by saying that "if we are to learn more about how leadership supports teachers in improving student outcomes, we need to measure how leaders attempt to influence the teaching practices that matter" (p. 669). This is a consideration echoed throughout the literature, the need for specific guidelines, instruments, and measurements to gauge the effectiveness of leadership behaviors.

Cultures of Learning and Learning Communities

Although the impact of professional learning communities and cultures of learning on school improvement is not a novel concept, the research has flourished in recent years. Edmonds (1982), Hauge et al. (2014), Hopkins (2001), Hopkins, Ainscow, and West (1994), Leithwood et al. (2008), and Reynolds et al. (1994), all linked forming learning teams and changing school culture as measures to increasing school effectiveness and improvement, but recent research has redefined and prioritized this process as instrumental to school improvement. Gruenert (2005), in seeking to clarify this concept, utilized the work of Hopkins et al. (1994) and described school cultures as

- The observed patterns of behavior, such as how teachers interact in the staff room, the language they use, and the rituals they establish.
- The norms that evolve in working groups of teachers in terms of lesson planning or monitoring the progress of students.
- The dominant values espoused by the school, typically through a mission statement.

- The philosophy that guides the approach to teaching and learning of particular subjects in a school.
- The unwritten policies and procedures that new teachers have to learn in order to get along in the school or their department. (Gruenert, 2005, p. 44)

The formation of school cultures, aligned to the above description, is a model mentioned throughout recent research in school improvement, as these cultures and communities operate as the space where school improvement conversations and movements are investigated, organized, and implemented most effectively (Benoliel & Berkovich, 2017; Dinham, Anderson, & Caldwell, 2011; DuFour, 2004; Emmett & Mcgee, 2012; Gruenert, 2005; Lambert, 2002; Mitchell & Sackney, 2016).

As early as 2004, DuFour acknowledged the trend of creating professional learning communities and sought to capture the structures that generated authentic professional learning communities and cultures that led to school improvement. DuFour (2004) emphasized that these structures exist for collaborative work and stated that "educators who are building a professional learning community recognize that they must work together to achieve their collective purpose of learning for all" (p. 9). DuFour (2004) also highlighted that learning communities regularly utilize assessments and data to inform future practice. These components of professional learning communities and cultures of learning are congruent with school improvement across the literature; namely creating the space for collaborative work and delegating assessment decisions across every level in a school district (Benoliel & Berkovich, 2017; DuFour, 2004; Goddard et al., 2007; Harris & DeFlaminis, 2016; Hughes & Kritsonis, 2006; Lambert, 2006; Sigurðardóttir & Sigþórsson, 2016). Muijs and Harris (2006) and Goddard et al. (2007) described these cultures as dependent upon mutual trust and support so that teachers can openly share instructional strategies, and feel empowered in their capacity to drive school initiatives with policy and assessment decisions. Mitchell and Sackney (2016) reported similar findings in high-capacity schools noting that within the learning communities and cultures of learning "the educators were held together by a common commitment to the well-being of the students, and they wanted to find effective ways to resolve their issues" (p. 864). When an atmosphere of respect, trust, support, and empowerment is created, school cultures are transformed and conditions for school improvement are generated (Dinham et al., 2011; Hughes & Kritsonis, 2006).

Learning communities and cultures of learning are emphasized throughout the research as the space for initiating school improvement; Lambert (2006) described this correlation by saying:

> Learning occurred in social groups, allowing participants to connect in new and complex ways, and thereby inspiring critical thought and energizing self-organization. When learning is continuous and participation in that learning is broad-based

and skillful, high leadership capacity and the potential of sustainable, lasting school improvement result. (p. 253)

Gruenert (2005) drew similar conclusions when discussing findings, stating that "collaborative cultures seem to be the best setting for student achievement, thus affirming the literature on collaborative school cultures" (p. 50). Benoliel and Berkovich (2017) reaffirmed this notion in their conclusion by identifying the influence of school teams and the necessity to promote inter/intra school relationships and collaboration when striving towards school improvement. Although the impactful role of professional learning communities and cultures of learning on school improvement is found across the research, there are also several overlapping considerations.

One consideration that was repeated throughout the literature was that this process of formulating learning communities and cultures is constant, cyclical, and perpetual (Emmett & Mcgee, 2012; Harris & DeFlaminis, 2016; Hughes & Kritsonis, 2006; Klar, Huggins, Hammonds, & Buskey, 2016; Sigurðardóttir & Sigþórsson, 2016). In light of this research, transitions in education, and fluctuating student body populations, researchers continually highlighted that cultures of learning are a process rather than a fixed state. Klar et al. (2016), in describing effective leadership, observed that supporting teachers and learning communities is a "cyclical process" (p. 132). Professional learning communities and cultures of learning were intertwined with school improvement when these communities reflected this continually developing model. An additional consideration is adequately incorporating parents, families, and support staff within these cultures and communities (Klar et al., 2016; Sigurðardóttir & Sigþórsson, 2016). Research regularly recognized that learning communities and cultures must include students, their families, and support staff so that the shared mission is truly shared throughout the community (Hughes & Kritsonis, 2006; Sigurðardóttir & Sigþórsson, 2016).

DISCUSSION

In the wake of NCLB and ESSA, education research has taken on a particular significance as states, districts, and schools grapple with addressing and meeting mandated stipulations. Reviewing research from the past two decades found that this influence is unmistakable, as practices, initiatives, and reforms highlighted as successful in developing and enabling school improvement regularly manifested themselves throughout countless schools nationwide, regardless of demographics and geography. To meet the challenges of legislation, resources were required, and educational research on school effectiveness and school improvement became those resources. School improvement plans and data practices, leadership behaviors, professional learning communities and cultures of learning, collaborative leadership, and distributed leadership were all interlinked with school improvement across the research, and correspondingly, these same concepts became the foundation of school improvement reforms within schools.

Although these concepts all link to school improvement, there is no static, patterned implementation that automatically instigates learning gains and proficient data growth. Rather, when these elements are simultaneously intertwined, continually developed, and demonstrated throughout all levels of a school, then the conditions are favorable for educational advances. According to the research, if a school cultivates a culture of learning or a professional learning community then simultaneously, the space for collaborative work is created. This space is an environment where staff can openly discuss their shared mission, nurture collaborative and distributed leadership, shape their school improvement plan, determine best data and accountability practices, and identify and develop efficacious instructional strategies and interventions (Benoliel & Berkovich, 2017; Dinham et al., 2011; DuFour, 2004; Emmett & Mcgee, 2012; Goddard et al., 2007; Gruenert, 2005; Hallinger & Heck, 2010; Harris & DeFlaminis, 2016; Hopkins, 2001; Lambert, 2002; Mitchell & Sackney, 2016; Sigurðardóttir & Sigþórsson, 2016); however, this process is constantly and continually developed, complex, and dependent upon an informed and committed staff; thus, it hinges upon a multitude of factors and contextual conditions that are reiterated throughout the research (Hassenpflug, 2013; Hopkins, 2001; Hughes & Kritsonis, 2006; Robinson et al., 2008).

In seeking to clarify the trends identified within school improvement research during the past two decades, a complicated relationship between policy and research begins to emerge. At times research is proactive and structures the policies. Instances of this include the required formation of school improvement plans and structured, strategic professional development and school reform initiatives. At other times, research is reactive to the legislation, such as the necessity of strict accountability measures imposed on schools and the explosion of literature on distributed and collaborative leadership structures to address the intricate process of analyzing and interpreting data to drive instruction. This ambiguous relationship between research and legislative reform causes contention at nearly every level as researchers, educators, and policymakers appear as separate entities competing for the ever-elusive prize of effective school improvement, when research has highlighted repeatedly that collaboration is the key to progress.

While developing a standardized set of practices, initiatives, and components that promote and initiate school improvement seems a logical end goal, it is more realistic to recognize that education is contextually bound and constantly fluctuating. Thus, practices, initiatives, and components understood to support school improvement need to reflect the context in which they are implemented as well as the need to be consistently and continually reframed and modified in light of developments and variations occurring within schools and society. This process is supported by ESSA and its emphasis on localized control. This process is also demanding at the local level, as administrators, department heads, and teacher leaders are responsible for identifying and implementing the practices and initiatives best suited to meet their needs; however, just as students are encouraged to develop and maintain growth mindsets, so too must educators if they are to genuinely work towards school improvement and a proficient student body population. Administrators and educators must remain reflective and open to restructuring their school improvement designs and reforms.

Fortunately, a shift in school improvement research has begun, namely that research now focuses largely on the local level. If research continues to be restricted to specific settings and focused on specific contextual factors then similar school environments can utilize and transfer those practices that nurtured school growth. Research is an invaluable resource, most recently due to studies which investigate and analyze specific school contexts and conditions. Findings from this research can then be generalized to similar schools that can utilize this research as a guide as they embark on their own school improvement journeys.

FURTHER RESEARCH

School improvement research must continue to emphasize investigating reforms, practices, and initiatives and their manifestations at the local level. The next phase of research should acknowledge and differentiate specific contextual settings, so that the research may serve as an implementation design for other schools. If researchers can build contextual maps that pinpoint and incorporate student demographics, school settings, staff dynamics, and other contextual factors for the local areas they investigate, then their findings may generalize as a guide for other schools.

Future research is needed to examine the complicated relationship between research, policy, and school reforms. Research is often proactive regarding policy, leading to the creation of new legislation. While at other times, research is reactive to policy, calling for new studies to address and investigate the demands set by policies. Research needs to analyze this dynamic and contradictory relationship to further clarify the impetus for school improvement—is it research, or is it policy? This research could potentially point out instances where research generated efficacious school improvement policy or vice-versa, and such findings could help shape the future of educational research.

A final area for further research, and this is a sentiment echoed throughout the literature, is the need to clarify and define specific terms associated with school improvement. Whether those terms are leadership behaviors, leadership styles, learning communities/cultures of learning, collaborative leadership, or distributed leadership, they need to be deconstructed so that they can be easily comprehended and serve as a pragmatic, specific means to achieve school improvement. Otherwise, these terms become meaningless when thrown into a school improvement plan only to be referenced during professional development.

CONCLUSION

There is no shortage of research on school improvement literature filled with not only pertinent findings and progressive reform strategies but also programs and reforms that are only successful on a small scale. We openly acknowledge the limitations of this study, as research from the past two decades could never fully encompass all the complexity affiliated with school improvement; however, the literature was clear that there are several factors that contribute to and facilitate school improvement. When schools create a culture of learning, are led by teachers and administrators with knowledge of contemporary pedagogical initiatives, and continually reflect on their mission and their practices, then school improvement results. This process is not linear or static, but cyclical and continually adapted and evolved in light of changes, context, and circumstances. As education moves forward, the relationship between researchers, policymakers, and educators needs to be negotiated and amalgamated. Since research repeatedly confirmed the value of collaborative work within a school, then this collaborative work should be carried out beginning at the legislative level, which, in turn, may lessen tensions and help create a culture of learning, rather than competition, both at the state and national level.

REFERENCES

Bennett, N., & Harvey, J. A. (2003). *Distributed leadership*. Nottingham: National College for School Leadership.

Benoliel, P., & Berkovich, I. (2017). There is no "I" in school improvement: The missing team perspective. *International Journal of Educational Management, 31*(7), 922–929. doi.org/10.1108/IJEM-04-2016-0069

Bolkan, S., & Holmgren, J. L. (2012). "You are such a great teacher and I hate to bother you but...": Instructors' perceptions of students and their use of email messages with varying politeness strategies. *Communication Education, 61*(3), 253–270. doi.org/10.1080/03634523.2012.667135

Darling-Hammond, L., Bae, S., Cook-Harvey, C. M., Lam, L., Mercer, C., Podolsky, A., & Stosich, E. L. (2016). *Pathways to new accountability through the Every Student Succeeds Act*. Palo Alto, CA: Learning Policy Institute.

Dimmock, C. (2012). Leadership of schools as research engage professional learning communities. In M. Brundrett & L. Bell (Eds.), *Leadership, capacity building and school improvement* (pp. 115–132). New York, NY: Routledge.

Dinham, S., Anderson, M., & Caldwell, B. (2011). Breakthroughs in school leadership development in Australia. *School Leadership & Management, 31*(2), 139–154. https://doi.org/10.1080/13632434.2011.560602

DuFour, R. (2004). What is a professional learning community? *Educational Leadership, 61*, 6–11. https://doi.org/10.1080/13674580500200380

Edmonds, R. R. (1982). *Research on teaching: Implications for practice*. Paper Presented at the National Invitational Conference of National Institute of Education. Washington DC.

Emmett, J., & Mcgee, D. (2012). A farewell to freshmen. *The Clearing House, 85*(2), 74–79. https://doi.org/10.1080/00098655.2011.619592

Elementary and Secondary Education Act of 1965. (1965). H.R. 2362, 89th Cong., 1st Sess., Public Law 89–10. Reports, Bills, Debate and Act.

Every Student Succeeds Act of 2015. (2015). Pub. L. No. 114-95 § 114 Stat. 1177.

Fairman, J. C., & Mackenzie, S. V. (2012). Spheres of teacher leadership action for learning. *Professional Development in Education, 38*(2), 229–246. https://doi.org/10.10 80/19415257.2012.657865

Fairman, J. C., & Mackenzie, S. V. (2015). How teacher leaders influence others and understand their leadership. *International Journal of Leadership in Education, 18*(1), 61–87. https://doi.org/10.1080/13603124.2014.904002

Goddard, Y. L., Goddard, R. D., & Tschannen-Moran, M. (2007). A theoretical and empirical investigation of teacher collaboration for school improvement and student achievement in public elementary schools. *Teachers College Record, 109*(4), 877–896.

Gray, J., Goldstein, H., & Thomas, S. (2003). Of trends and trajectories: Searching for patterns in school improvement. *British Educational Research Journal, 29*(1), 83–88. https://doi.org/10.1080/0141192032000057393

Gruenert, S. (2005). Correlations of collaborative school cultures with student achievement. *NASSP Bulletin, 89*(645), 43–55. https://doi.org/10.1177/019263650508964504

Hallinger, P., & Heck, R. H. (2010). Leadership for learning: Does collaborative leadership make a difference in school improvement? *Educational Management Administration and Leadership, 38*(6), 654–678. https://doi.org/10.1177/1741143210379060

Harris, A. (2004). Distributed leadership and school improvement. *Educational Management Administration & Leadership, 32*(1), 11–24. https://doi.org/10.1177/1741143204039297

Harris, A., & DeFlaminis, J. (2016). Distributed leadership in practice: Evidence, misconceptions and possibilities. *Management in Education, 30*(4), 141–146. https://doi.org/10.1177/0892020616656734

Hassenpflug, A. (2013). How to improve instructional leadership : High school principal selection process versus evaluation process. *The Clearing House: A Journal of Educational Strategies, Issues and Ideas, 86*(3), 90–92. https://doi.org/10.1080/000986 55.2012.755147

Hauge, T. E., Norenes, S. O., & Vedøy, G. (2014). School leadership and educational change: Tools and practices in shared school leadership development. *Journal of Educational Change, 15*(4), 357–376. https://doi.org/10.1007/s10833-014-9228-y

Heck, R. H., & Hallinger, P. (2010). Testing a longitudinal model of distributed leadership effects on school improvement. *Leadership Quarterly, 21*(5), 867–885. https://doi.org/10.1016/j.leaqua.2010.07.013

Hopkins, D. (2001). *School improvement for real.* New York: Routledge Falmer. https://doi.org/10.4324/9780203165799

Hopkins, D., Ainscow, M., & West, M. (1994). *School Improvement in an era of change.* London, UK: Cassell.

House, J. (2014). Funding survival toolkit NCLB Waivers : Good news and bad news. *T H E Journal,* (February 2013), 8–11.

Hughes, T. A., & Kritsonis, W. A. (2006). A national perspective: An exploration of professional learning communities and the impact on school improvement efforts. *Doctoral Forum*, *1*(1), 1–12.

Jean-Marie, G., Normore, A. H., & Brooks, J. S. (2009). Leadership for social justice: Preparing 21st century school leaders for a new social order. *Journal of Research on Leadership Education*, *4*(1), 1–31. https://doi.org/10.1177/194277510900400102

Johnson, L., & Sillman, K. (2012). When the leader leaves: Sustaining success at Romero High School. *Journal of Cases in Educational Leadership*, *15*(3), 47–55. https://doi.org/10.1177/1555458912447847

Kaniuka, T. S. (2012). Toward an understanding of how teachers change during school reform: Considerations for educational leadership and school improvement. *Journal of Educational Change*, *13*(3), 327–346. https://doi.org/10.1007/s10833-012-9184-3

Kelly, A., & Saunders, N. (2010). New heads on the block: three case studies of transition to primary school headship. *School Effectiveness and School Improvement*, *30*(2), 127–142. https://doi.org/10.1080/13632431003663180

Klar, H. W., Huggins, K. S., Hammonds, H. L., & Buskey, F. C. (2016). Fostering the capacity for distributed leadership: A post-heroic approach to leading school improvement. *International Journal of Leadership in Education*, *19*(2), 111–137. https://doi.org/10.1080/13603124.2015.1005028

Lambert, L. (2002). A framework for shared leadership. *Educational Leadership*, *59*(8), 3740.

Lambert, L. (2003). *Leadership capacity for lasting school improvement*. Alexandria, VA: Assoc. for Supervision and Curriculum Development.

Lambert, L. (2006). Lasting leadership: A study of high leadership capacity schools. *Educational Forum*, *70*(3), 238–254. https://doi.org/10.1080/00131720608984900

Leithwood, K. (2016). Department-head leadership for school improvement. *Leadership and Policy in Schools*, *15*(2), 117–140. https://doi.org/10.1080/15700763.2015.1044538

Leithwood, K., Harris, A., & Hopkins, D. (2008). Seven strong claims about successful school leadership. *School Leadership and Management*, *28*(1), 27–42. https://doi.org/10.1080/13632430701800060

Leithwood, K., Louis, K. S., Anderson, S., & Wahlstrom, K. (2009). *Second international handbook of educational change*. Paper presented at The Wallace Foundation Center for Applied Research and Educational Improvement and Ontario Institute for Studies in Education New York NY, 2007(October 20, pp. 1–90). https://doi.org/10.1007/978-90-481-2660-6

Louis, K. S. (2015). Linking leadership to learning: state, district and local effects. *Nordic Journal of Studies in Educational Policy*, *2015*(3), 30321. https://doi.org/10.3402/nstep.v1.30321

Marks, W. (2013). Leadership succession and retention, it is time to get serious about a principal retention policy. *Leading and Managing*, *19*(2), 1–14.

Mills, J. (2008). A legislative overview of No Child Left Behind. *New Directions for Higher Education*, (117), 9–20. https://doi.org/10.1002/ev

Mitchell, C., & Sackney, L. (2016). School improvement in high-capacity schools: Educational leadership and living-systems ontology. *Educational Management Administration and Leadership*, *44*(5), 853–868. https://doi.org/10.1177/1741143214564772

Moher, D., Shamseer, L., Clarke, M., Ghersi, D., Liberati, A., Petticrew, M., ... Stewart, L. (2015). Preferred reporting items for systematic review and meta-analysis protocols (PRISMA-P) 2015 statement. *Systematic Reviews, 4*(1), 1–19.

Muijs, D., & Harris, A. (2006). Teacher led school improvement: Teacher leadership in the UK. *Teaching and Teacher Education, 22*(8), 961–972. https://doi.org/10.1016/j.tate.2006.04.010

Murphy, J. (2015). Forces shaping schooling and school leadership. *Journal of School Leadership, 25*(November 2015), 1056–1087.

No Child Left Behind Act of 2001, P.L. 107–110, 20 U.S.C. § 6319 (2002).

O'Day, J. A. (2002). Complexity, accountability, and school improvement. *Harvard Educational Review, 72*(3), 293–330. Retrieved from http://proxy.library.upenn.edu:3341/content/021q742t8182h238/fulltext.pdf

Reynolds, D., Sammons, P., Fraine, B. De, Damme, J. Van, Teddlie, C., Stringfield, S., ... Stringfield, S. (2014). Educational effectiveness research (EER): A state- of-the-art review. *School Effectiveness and School Improvement, 25*(2), 197–230. https://doi.org/10.1080/09243453.2014.885450

Reynolds, D., Teddlie, C., Creemers, B. P. M., Cheng, Y. C., Dundas, B., Green, B., ... Stringfield, S. (1994). School effectiveness research: A review of the international literature. In *Advances in school effectiveness research and practice*. Tarrytown, NY: Elsevier Science Inc.

Robinson, V. M. J., Lloyd, C. A., & Rowe, K. J. (2008). The impact of leadership on student outcomes: An analysis of the differential effects of leadership types. *Educational Administration Quarterly, 44*(5), 635–674. https://doi.org/10.1177/0013161X08321509

Saldana, J. (2013). *The coding manual for qualitative researchers*. Thousand Oaks, CA: SAGE Publications.

Saultz, A., Fusarelli, L. D., & McEachin, A. (2017). The Every Student Succeeds Act, the decline of the federal role in education policy, and the curbing of executive authority. *Publius, 47*(3), 426–444. https://doi.org/10.1093/publius/pjx031

Sigurðardóttir, S. M., & Sigþórsson, R. (2016). The fusion of school improvement and leadership capacity in an elementary school. *Educational Management Administration and Leadership, 44*(4), 599–616. https://doi.org/10.1177/1741143214559230

Spillane, J. P., Halverson, R:, & Diamond, J. B. (2001). Investigating school leadership practice: A distributed perspective. *Educational Researcher, 30*(3), 23–28. https://doi.org/10.3102/0013189X030003023

CHAPTER 4

RESEARCH TRENDS IN SCHOOL IMPROVEMENT FOR MARGINALIZED STUDENTS

James A. Martinez

Schools improve when purpose and effort unite . . . one key is leadership that recognizes its most vital function: to keep everyone's eyes on the prize of improved student learning.

—*Schmoker (1999, p. 111)*

CONTEXTUAL DEFINITION OF MARGINALIZED STUDENTS

As stated in its official charter (American Educational Research Association, 2018), the purpose of the Leadership for School Improvement (LSI) Special Interest Group (SIG) of the American Educational Research Association is to "examine how leadership of teachers, principals and superintendents influences instructional capacity (results) in improved student outcomes . . . encourag(ing) discussion and development of the philosophical, theoretical and empirical tenets guiding school and system renewal" (para.1). In keeping with the purpose of the LSI SIG, this chapter will focus on how schools and school systems have addressed the needs

---

Leadership for School Improvement: Reflection and Renewal
pages 53–65.
Copyright © 2019 by Information Age Publishing
All rights of reproduction in any form reserved.

of marginalized students. Both instructional and non-instructional (i.e., programmatic) methods to achieve this aim will be provided. Research studies accepted for publication between 2001 and 2017 in peer-reviewed, scholarly journals were reviewed, specifically those that focused on school improvement to support not only the academic, but the socio-emotional lives of marginalized students.

Policy considerations, while important, will not be the primary focus of this chapter but rather the degree that school accountability measures implemented by schools and school districts as a result of measures associated with the No Child Left Behind Act (NCLB) has affected the manner in which marginalized students are served and monitored. The earliest research used in this study corresponds with the passing of NCLB by the U.S. Congress in 2001 and subsequently signed into law in early 2002.

Prior to discussion of this research, I identify which students in today's schools are considered *marginalized*. A number of personal, behavioral, social, learning and family conditions are noteworthy. These would include (in no particular order, and not limited to) students identified with/as: (a) low socioeconomic status (SES), including those who are family wage earners, (b) non/limited English speaking, (c) migrants/homeless/ refugee status, (d) learning disabilities, (e) emotional disorders, (f) physical disabilities, (g) cognitive impairments, (h) intellectual disabilities (InD), (i) physically abused or suffering other types of physical/emotional trauma, (j) LGBTQ, (k) chronic substance abuse, (l) from homes with a lack of access to educational resources, including adequate technology, (m) from foster homes, single-parent homes or not being raised by parents, (n) placed in one or more curricular tracks, (o) from military families, (p) limited association with mentoring persons, (q) first-generation college students, (r) from homes with contrasting socio-cultural norms, and (s) being raised by persons who are incarcerated or have been previously incarcerated. To explore the instructional leadership practices that improve student outcomes for students represented in all these categories would be a mammoth undertaking, especially within the limits of this chapter; however, an investigation of factors that relate to instruction of students with InD, from low SES families, and/or attending schools in both rural and innercity (i.e., urban) environments will serve to begin the discussion.

METHODOLOGY

Moher et al. (2015) stated that systematic reviews are undertaken as an attempt to "collate all relevant evidences that fits pre-specified eligibility criteria to answer a specific research question" (p. 3). The Educational Research Information Center, Academic Search Complete, and Education Source databases were searched using the terms *school improvement, at-risk, underrepresented* and *marginalized* in the text of submitted abstracts of peer-reviewed journals.

Over 150 articles, books, and reports were reviewed. Essays and literature reviews were also included, as well as articles submitted by authors outside the United States, including Australia and Canada. Articles identified through the search engines that did not address the specific criteria of the study were omitted from the search, including all those which were focused on higher education (e.g., college/university). After excluding articles that did not specifically address both marginalized students and school improvement efforts, 25 articles remained. For this subset of articles, a matrix was developed in a Microsoft Excel spreadsheet which identified: (a) the author(s) and date of publication, (b) the specific marginalized group(s) studied, (c) any intervention(s) that were performed on target group(s), and (d) relevant findings. Topics included in this reduced set of articles included intervention models, targeted programs, curricular reforms, as well as ethnographic and case studies. Additionally, a wide range of qualitative research studies were included, adding those with action research and narrative methodological designs, as well as other studies that gathered interview and observation data. After the literature search, a thorough review of each of the articles was completed, and descriptive, handwritten notes were added to the spreadsheet which identified the article type (e.g., research, opinion piece), type of K–12 school/school system (e.g., urban, rural, public private, elementary, secondary), and a description of specific intervention/program (if any). Creswell (2012) described this manner of investigation as "preliminary exploratory analysis . . . consist(ing) of exploring the data to obtain a general sense of (it)" (p. 243).

This review of the literature revealed a variety of ways that schools and the leaders that serve these schools addressed the needs of marginalized student over the past two decades, including efforts focused on (a) social justice (6 references), (b) urban considerations (8 references), and (c) interventions/programs (6 references). Due to the substantive nature of ideas discovered as a result of this targeted review, each of the aforementioned themes will be highlighted in relation to school improvement of marginalized populations. To include historical context to the discussions, publication dates will be noted throughout as well. Although limited in scope, this chapter will provide a systematic review of efforts revealed, providing a basis for understanding the trends related to leadership practices that aspire to serve marginalized students.

FINDINGS

Social Justice Considerations

The degree to which educational leaders provide equitable access to resources for marginalized students is connected to concepts of social justice. As early as the 1920s and 1930s, American psychologist John Dewey established ideas related to democratic reform in relation to educational settings. Furman (2004) stated that " . . . educational leadership is fundamentally a moral endeavour . . . " (p. 215). Furthermore, she stated that "working for social justice requires a deliberate intervention that challenges fundamental inequities and works toward better educational and economic outcomes for marginalized children" (Furman, 2004, p. 228). As part of this study, a number of peer-reviewed journal articles published between 2007 and 2013 connected aspects of social justice to addressing the needs of marginalized students. These articles presented evidence that related to educational leaders' efforts to address injustice in schools, including changing normative beliefs about children, formally incorporating culturally relevant pedagogical practices, instituting program elements to create a school climate that focuses on welcoming families of marginalized students, and implementing a "social justice approach" as part of a school improvement plan (SIP).

Ullucci (2007) advocated for educators to change normative beliefs for children of color, English language learners (ELLs) and children from low SES families. The argument centered on *unspoken and unchallenged* beliefs that affect practice and policy in schools, cemented to propagate the status quo. Furthermore, Ullucci promoted the idea that regardless of improvements to *tangible changes* for students (e.g., access to technology, improved textbooks, increases in instructional aides), attention to changing inequitable normative beliefs among teachers is more *fundamental*. It is "reconceptualizing beliefs about race, merit and fairness" (Ullucci, 2007, p. 2) that lies at the core of social justice reform that needs to be prioritized in schools. Specifically targeted should be *blame shifting myths* that undermine teacher motivations to equitably support needy students, promoting the notion that these students' families do not support educational efforts.

Ullucci (2007) also addressed the *myth of meritocracy*, the notion that all students have equal opportunity to succeed, both personally and academically, based on their personal work ethic. The author's contention is that

> Teachers who support the notion of meritocracy set up a worthy/unworthy dichotomy. Because all students have equal chances to excel, students who do succeed within the system are worthy of the benefits they receive. Children who fail do so of their own accord, not because of bias in the system. The myth of meritocracy is also colorblind. Merit stresses individual student efforts while minimizing race and language based factors. (Ullucci, 2007, p. 4)

Finally, Ullucci (2007) highlighted the issue of *colorblindness* among educators—owing to their inability to equitably address the unique educational needs of students of color. She stated that "one that treats all children equally and is devoid of bias is disingenuous. When teachers operationalize colorblindness in classrooms, however well-intended, the consequences are damaging" (Ullucci, 2007, p. 4). This article provided a motivational foundation for educational reform, outlining the need for educators to take notice of their own attitudes and beliefs that diminish their ability to support marginalized students.

Having now established the foundations for educational change to better support marginalized students, the realities of social justice reform in schools, as experienced by site administrators who have attempted to implement these changes, are important to understand. The trials and tribulations experienced by educational leaders in the latter part of the first decade of the 21st century highlight what is required, both personally and professionally, in serving marginalized students at that time.

Theoharis (2007) provided ample evidence of these difficulties experienced by school leaders, reflecting on research that used a case study research design. He interviewed seven school principals who "came to the principalship with a social justice orientation, who make issues of race, class, gender, disability, sexual orientation, and other historically marginalizing factors central to their . . . leadership practice . . . and who have demonstrated success in making their schools more just" (Theoharis, 2007, p. 221). To further involve himself in the study and conform to an autoethnographical methodology, the author included himself as one of the subjects.

To enact social justice, these principals, through a variety of strategies, focused on (a) raising student achievement, (b) improving school structures, (c) enhancing staff capacity, and (d) strengthening school culture and community. Specific interventions were intended to support a diverse group of students (e.g., ethnicity, SES) involved in a variety of programs, including special education and English Language Development. As a result of these efforts, participation at school events by marginalized families increased at all sites. Hindering this progress at every school, however, were apathetic staff members who strongly resisted the interventions. In addition, limited funds made it difficult for the principals at many of the schools to provide needy students with additional resources to support their learning.

Central office obstacles included "unsupportive central office administrators, a formidable bureaucracy, prosaic colleagues, . . . harmful state and federal regulations, and uninspired administrator preparation" (Theoharis, 2007, p. 240). Principals in the study used proactive and coping strategies (e.g., not discussing work after leaving their sites) to offset the extreme physical, mental, and emotional toll they experienced while enacting social justice efforts at their schools. Theoharis (2007) concluded his study by recommending that administrator preparation programs include specific training to better prepare educational leaders for the difficulties they will encounter in transforming schools with regard to social justice.

Theoharis (2010) furthered his research by immersing himself in the same six schools, not including his own, for a full school year to better understand those site administrators who "possessed a belief that promoting social justice is a driving force behind what brought them to their leadership position" (p. 331). He found that the principals in this study encountered, and worked to disrupt, four types of school injustices that adversely affected marginalized students at their sites. These included "school structures that marginalize, segregate, and impede achievement, such as pullout programs; a deprofessionalized teaching staff who could benefit from focused staff development; a school climate that needed to be more welcoming to marginalized families and the community; and disparate student achievement levels" (Theoharis, 2010, p. 332).

According to Theoharis (2010), eliminating pullout programs for special education students, those identified as ELLs and students segregated for mathematics was "central to giving students access to richer curriculum and instruction" (p. 343). To combat issues of race on their campuses, the principals in the study led whole-staff conversations about inequities in the classroom for students with differing ethnicities. Hiring and supervision policies were adapted to ensure that employees at the school sites were in agreement with social justice efforts. Finally, the principals made efforts to make their schools inviting for marginalized families by creating a welcoming climate, creating opportunities to reach out to these families and incorporating aspects of social responsibility into the school curriculum.

In the end, the goal of increasing academic achievement among students of color and those from low SES families by direct and indirect measures permeated these school leaders' everyday efforts. Gains were recorded for marginalized students in a variety of measures, including increased student attendance, course passing and graduation rates, increased parent involvement, and positive interac-

TABLE 4.1. Pros and Cons of Reallocating Resources to Support New Programs

Pros—Reallocating Resources to Support New Program	Cons—Reallocating Resources to Support New Program
The most at-risk students will have their needs met and the potential to achieve their own definition success.	May weaken relationships with some teaching staff; teachers affected by these changes may decide to apply to work at other schools during school staffing.
Continuity in progress and success of School Improvement Plan.	May create conflict among teachers (some may support SIP's new initiative and the reallocation of resources, others may not).
May impress superintendent with commitment to SIP and social justice.	Some students may miss out on opportunities due to reallocation of resources.
More likely to meet long term goal of improving the community.	Potential backlash from some parents if their child loses out because of these changes.
Pros—Not Reallocating Resources to Support New Program	**Cons—Not Reallocating Resources to Support New Program**
Gain further trust/respect of staff by demonstrating a willingness to include them in important decisions.	Disappoint/lose the trust of at-risk students that have started to buy in to their unique chance at success; disappoint/lose trust of those students' parents
More time to work on other principal tasks.	Stagnate the progress of SIP.
Eliminate stress associated with trying to begin a new program.	Students are those that lose out due to issues outside their control (tension among staff).
Avoid conflict with staff by "not rocking the boat."	Potential backlash from superintendent due to limited progress with SIP.

Note: Higginbottom (2013)

tions with staff. Theoharis (2010) concluded his work with these school leaders by stating that

> Although the sample studied here represented but a small group of principals from a small number of urban schools, it provided good examples of real possibilities for improving the education of our most marginalized students. These leaders held onto the idealism that social justice in schools is a necessary ongoing struggle, and with that idealism, they achieved results. (p. 369)

Higginbottom (2013) observed site principal activities of social justice measures as part of a SIP which included progressive reform measures that reallocated resources to support marginalized students. As the average income among the 600 families was approximately $68,000 and there were very few minorities and no English as a second language students attending the school, the principal focused on students who were struggling academically and not involved in co-curricular activities who were, in his opinion, involved in the sale and distribution of illegal drugs.

This case study illuminates potential obstacles that school leaders face when focusing on the needs of marginalized students, when considering the needs of non-marginalized students, given a fixed expense budget. Decisions for use of federal funding would have been accomplished by a School Site Council committee made up of parents, teachers, staff, and administrator(s). Higginbottom (2013) provided a chart that expresses the pros and cons related to reallocating resources to support marginalized students, reproduced for this chapter in Table 4.1.

URBAN CONSIDERATIONS

Normore, Rodriguez, and Wynne (2007) stated "far less likely are opportunities for urban . . . people to engage in educational initiatives that create opportunities to study their experiences, share their knowledge . . . that are most relevant to the realities facing their lives, both in education and beyond" (p. 667). Factoring into an educational leader's decision making process is the geographic context of their school(s). As it relates to poverty and educational resource distribution, it is important to "acknowledg(e) the spatial distribution of economic disadvantage (in) evaluating the impact of policy across more and less disadvantaged areas" (Irving, 2008, p. 606). Although contextrelated issues in rural and suburban schools deserve due consideration, the systematic review revealed a plethora of articles that focused on urban schools, which describe insights by site administrators, aspects of resistance to reform, and curricular interventions in urban schools.

Jacobson, Brooks, Giles, Johnson, and Ylimaki (2007) examined the efforts of three new principals serving students in high poverty, urban elementary schools in New York State. The selection of the principals for the study was based on an investigation of increased state assessment scores from administrators. Three African American, female principals were interviewed and focus group interviews were conducted at each site with parents and students. Although each principal exhibited a different style of leadership, the interviews revealed a common set of professional attributes for the administrators at each site, including setting high expectations for student behavior and academic achievement, making efforts to ensure the campuses were safe and welcoming, and increased visibility of the administrator on the school grounds during each school day. The principals "recognized the barriers to learning and academic achievement that poverty can produce, but none would allow these conditions to be used as excuses for poor performance" (Jacobson et al., 2007, p. 310).

Urban schools have been described as *reform-proof*, owing to a number of impediments to change. The schools experiencing the most difficulties

> suffer from deeply rooted cultures of failure and distrust, are politically conflicted, personality driven and racially tense, have difficulty learning from their own experiences or that of others, have difficulty communicating internally, have difficulty following through even when they achieve consensus about what to do, have shallow pools of relevant professional skill, unstable staffs, and exist in a larger institutional environment that is itself unstable and ill-equipped to do much more than issue mandates and threats. (Payne & Kaba, 2007, p. 37)

In a multi-year, action research project conducted with the cooperation of a low-performing, high poverty, urban elementary school in Toronto, Canada, Cooper and White (2006) targeted student deficiencies in reading by implementing a *critical literacy* program. Obstacles to implementing specific interventions came, not with the students but with teachers who had difficulty "helping to construct their students' identities through the beliefs they carry about who the students are and what they believe the students are capable of" (Cooper & White, 2006, p. 88). A year later, Deno et al. (2008) published results of a curriculum-based measurement tool as a reading intervention to support students in an urban elementary school in a large, Midwestern city. Although the intervention was applied to all students, specific subgroups were targeted, including "students at risk, students who are non-native English speakers, and students with special needs" (Deno et al., 2008, p. 44). Results of this study showed that "when school-wide implementation occurs, it becomes possible to compare the growth of different subgroups of students [which is] particularly important with the advent of NCLB and the mandate that districts monitor their lowest subgroups" (Deno et al., 2008, p. 51).

Related ethnographical research substantiates the idea that gifted African American students in urban high schools who have consistent support by *significant others* in their homes and communities develop social networks which bolster their success (Graham & Anderson, 2008). In a more recent study, Bukoski, Lewis, Carpenter, Berry, and Sanders (2015) interviewed nine assistant principals serving in urban, low-achieving high schools in a Midwestern U.S. city regarding the degree to which community partnerships developed through the use of Title I School Improvement Grants could be utilized to support marginalized students. Prior to data collection, "the researchers assumed many of the assistant principals in this study would reveal their displeasure for the School Improvement Grants because they were tied to turnaround measures of the No Child Left Behind Act" (Bukoski et al., 2015, p. 424). To their surprise, the assistant principals communicated strong connections between measures funded by SIPs and connections to local communities, which in turn supported marginalized students at their sites.

In a more recent case-study by Kirk et al. (2017), groups of ELLs from an ethnically diverse, urban public high school located in a Midwestern United States city served as participants to determine the degree to which the school climate endorsed *student empowerment*. Observations as well as individual and focus group interviews were used for data collection for a single academic semester. The participating school served a variety of marginalized students, including "more than three out of four (who) were 'economically disadvantaged' and . . . almost one in four . . . designated as 'English Language Learners'" (Kirk et al., 2017, p. 833). The results of the study led the researchers to develop a Student Empowerment Model which "affected by individual characteristics (e.g., personality, learning abilities, etc.), ecological contexts (e.g., family, neighborhood), and the characteristics of empowering classrooms and schools, leads to empowered outcomes (intrapersonal, interactional, and behavioral)" (Kirk et al., 2017, p. 833). Anderson-Butcher, Iachini, Ball, Barke, and Martin (2016) confirmed the importance of focusing on students in urban schools, stating "in urban communities, where there are often large numbers of students of racial and ethnic diversity and of students who live in poverty, the complexity of these issues can become even more challenging" (p. 190).

Interventions and Programs

According to Normore et al. (2007), "while all children have a constitutional right to an education according to State law, not all children receive an equitable opportunity to learn, particularly for Black, Latina/o and other marginalized children in US society" (p. 667). One strategy of reforming schools for the betterment of marginalized students and their families is the implementation of targeted interventions that can affect academic and/or social outcomes. A number of these interventions have been used with students from more than one site, and several (e.g., The Comer Model, The Corrective Reading Program, The Movement Model, The Children First Initiative, The Real World Literacy Project, among others) have been formalized for general use, depending on the specific needs of the school/school district. While not all of these more formalized interventions will be detailed in this section, a few that have been used to target the needs of marginalized students, as well as other which have been customized for a particular school/school district will be highlighted.

To target the specialized needs of immigrant students and their families, Johns (2001) highlighted the prescribed components of the Comer Model, a school development program to promote positive and constructive stakeholder relationships for schools. This child-centered, holistic approach includes the construction and use of teams (i.e., parent; school planning and management; school, staff, and support) in cooperation with staff development and assessment efforts to fulfill obligations of guiding principles. All this is accomplished through the development of the SIP, a required element prescribed by NCLB mandates. Serving as an autoethnographer, Johns provided rich descriptions of the implementation of the Comer Model at her site while serving as a teacher for four years and later as an educational consultant. Johns (2001) concluded her essay by noting that "The Comer School Development Program has a structure, philosophy, focus, and perspective that is universally applicable and can help parents have a voice in meeting the education needs of their children" (p. 273).

Interventions implemented in schools outside the U.S. show promise to positively affect student outcomes. Boxma, Maxwell, and Weeks (2009) detailed the implementation of a "Real World Literacy Project" at a rural elementary school in Alberta, Canada. The intervention included:

> cross-grade, cross-curricular theme inquiry based units... which would consciously try to incorporate the skills... crucial for student success in 21st century participatory culture, namely play performance, simulation, appropriation, multitasking, distributed cognition, collective intelligence, judgement, transmedia navigation, networking and negotiation. (Boxma et al., 2009, p. 562)

Student survey results collected at the end of the intervention showed increased enthusiasm for learning by participating students, and increased satisfaction by parents.

In another, single-site intervention, low-performing elementary school students (i.e., 30th percentile in reading, mathematics, and writing in state and district assessments) from a low-SES U.S. elementary school participated in a multi-tier Schoolwide Enrichment Model. The intervention included differentiated instruction strategies, Writer's Workshop and Global Studies curricular components, and an after-school academic support program (Beecher, 2010). As in the previous instance, the participating students from a variety of ethnic backgrounds showed academic gains, as well as improvements in student attitudes about school and learning.

Research involving specific interventions that target marginalized student needs which are implemented across a group of schools in a school district were also included in this systematic review of literature. Anderson-Butcher et al. (2010) described the implementation of an 18-month community collaboration model, focusing on teachers, support staff, and school leaders at six failing elementary schools in an urban Ohio school district. The intervention included cross-site professional development and networking sessions as well as substantive funding for substitute teachers which allowed educators to attend off-site trainings. Although the interventions were targeted directly at persons who either directly or indirectly supported students, student reading scores for each grade level increased, except for males, economically disadvantaged, and, in certain grade levels, those without disabilities and Whites. Of all the interventions investigated, this study revealed the degree that certain subgroups, marginalized and not, would not necessarily benefit from a school-wide reform.

A research-validated, remedial reading intervention program was used to target the *most at-risk* third through fifth grade students in a historically low-performing elementary school in a low-SES neighborhood (Kaniuka, 2012). Using a case study approach, teacher reflections were gathered before (during related professional development), during, and after implementation of the program. The program was initiated as a review of potential reading intervention models by the teachers which showed promise to address struggling students at their school. Ultimately, the teachers chose Corrective Reading as the program they would implement at their school. Results showed significant improvements in self-efficacy related to teachers' perceptions of capacity and commitment as the study progressed. This study reveals the extent that buy in and substantive professional development have on the success of intervention programs, for both teachers and marginalized students.

DISCUSSION

As a whole, the articles outlined from 2001 to 2017 provided evidence of the research, published in the U.S. and abroad, that has been conducted to highlight measures of support for marginalized populations. Connections to measures that have affected school accountability and funding as a result of NCLB have been highlighted to better understand how federal reforms are connected to educational aims for these students. From social justice to community context (i.e., urban) considerations, research is focused on what was happening in the profiled schools that affects these students. From local to more broadly implemented interventions, research focused on the ways that targeted programs are effective in serving needy students, their families, and communities. As was stated in the opening paragraphs, it is not the intent of this article to fully represent all research on this topic, but this modest review serves as a catalyst for conversations about how best to serve marginalized students in an era of accountability.

Cumulatively, the articles reviewed serve to reinforce the importance of teachers' understandings of student learning capacity, based on stereotypes related to SES, race, parent involvement, and associated factors. Countering deficit thinking among those involved in the education of marginalized students is crucial to improving the academic and social lives of these needy students. Implementing interventions that are selected by those who will implement them and providing engaging, substantive professional development before, during, and after implementation will ensure, to the degree possible, that targeted reforms are successful.

FURTHER RESEARCH

A number of areas that were not addressed in this chapter are worth further investigation. Leadership that focuses on supporting students culturally, both in and out of the classroom, is receiving more and more attention as some students and their families are increasingly mobile. Ladson-Billings (2009) stated that "culturally relevant teaching honors the students' sense of humanity and dignity" (p. 82). Clearly, leaders who devise culturally relevant pedagogical practices will need to take student backgrounds and experiences into account in supporting their teachers serving a more diverse student body. Also, a broader search of literature, with regard to key words, databases used, and timeframe, will allow for increased perspectives on the topic of supporting marginalized students.

CONCLUSION

Comer (1987) stated that "improving the education of high risk children is one of the most important tasks facing our nation" (p. 13). The intention of this investigation was to provide a systematic review of studies, revealing the trends, policies, and practices associated with serving marginalized students.

Educators, from classroom and resource teachers, administrators, and parents, to name a few, can contribute to future efforts. Darling-Hammond (1997) wrote that "non-teaching personnel constitute more than half the US education workforce . . . (who) are supposed to design, plan and monitor the work of teachers" (pp. 40–41). Regardless of the support provided to instructional leaders in or out of the classroom, improving instruction is an important aspect in addressing the academic (and as a result, social-emotional) needs of today's students.

REFERENCES

American Educational Research Association. (2018). *Leadership for school improvement SIG 101*. Retrieved from http://www.aera.net/SIG101/Leadership-for-School-Improvement-SIG-101

Anderson-Butcher, D., Iachini, A. L., Lawson, H., Flaspohler, P., Bean, J., & WadeMdivanian, R. (2010). Emergent evidence in support of a community collaboration model for school improvement. *Children & Schools, 32*(3), 160–171.

Anderson-Butcher, D., Iachini, A. L., Ball, A., Barke, S., & Martin, L. D. (2016). A university–school partnership to examine the adoption and implementation of the Ohio community collaboration model in one urban school district: A mixed-method case study. *Journal of Education for Students Placed At Risk, 21*(3), 190–204.

Beecher, M. (2010). Schoolwide enrichment model: Challenging all children to excel. *Gifted Education International, 26*, 177–191.

Bukoski, B. E., Lewis, T. C., Carpenter, B. W., Berry, M. S., & Sanders, K. S. (2015). The complexities of realizing community: Assistant principals as community leaders in persistently low-achieving schools. *Leadership and Policy in Schools, 14*, 411–436.

Boxma, A., Maxwell, N., & Weeks, P. (2009). Does a 'flat world' level the playing field? *The International Journal of Learning, 16*(11), 557–567.

Comer, J. P. (1987). New Haven's school-community connection. *Educational Leadership, 44*(6), 13–16.

Cooper, K., & White, R. E. (2006). Action research in practice: Critical literacy in an urban grade 3 classroom. *Educational Action Research, 14*(1), 83–99.

Creswell, J. W. (2012). *Educational research: Planning, conducting, and evaluating quantitative and qualitative research.* Boston, MA: Pearson.

Darling-Hammond, L. (1997). *The right to learn: A blueprint for creating schools that work.* San Francisco, CA: Jossey-Bass.

Deno, S. L, Reschly, A. L., Lembke, E. S., Magnusson, D., Callender, S. A., Windram, H., & Stachel, N. (2008). Developing a school-wide progress-monitoring system. *Psychology in the Schools, 46*(1), 44–55.

Furman, G. C. (2004). The ethic of community. *Journal of Educational Administration, 42*(2), 215–235. https://doi.org/10.1108/09578230410525612

Graham, A., & Anderson, K. A. (2008). "I have to be three steps ahead": Academically gifted African American male students in an urban high school on the tension between an ethnic and academic identity. *Urban Review, 40*(1), 472–499.

Higginbottom, K. (2013). Social justice in schools: A case of conflicting values. *Canadian Journal of Educational Administration, 142*(1), 120–133.

Irving, S. K. (2008). State welfare rules, TANF exits, and geographic context: Does place matter? *Rural Sociology, 73*(4), 605–630.

Jacobson, S. L., Brooks, S., Giles, C., Johnson, L. & Ylimaki, R. (2007). Successful leadership in three high-poverty urban elementary schools. *Leadership and Policy in Schools, 6,* 291–317.

Johns, S. E. (2001). Using the Comer Model to educate immigrant children. *Childhood Education, 77*(5), 268–274.

Kaniuka, T. S. (2012). Toward an understanding of how teachers change during school reform: Considerations for educational leadership and school improvement. *Journal of Educational Change, 13,* 327–346.

Kirk, C. M., Lewis, R. K., Brown, K., Karibo, B., Scott, A., & Park, E. (2017). The empowering schools project: Identifying the classroom and school characteristics that lead to student empowerment. *Youth & Society, 49*(6), 827–847.

Ladson-Billings, G. J. (2009). *The dreamkeepers: Successful teachers of African American children.* San Francisco, CA: Jossey-Bass.

Moher, D., Shamseer, L., Clarke, M., Ghersi, D., Liberati, A., Pettigrew, M., ... Stewart, L. (2015). Preferred reporting items for systematic review and meta-analysis protocols (PRISMA-P) 2015 statement. *Systematic Reviews, 4*(1), 1–19.

Normore, A. H., Rodriguez, L., & Wynne, J. (2007). Making all children winners: Confronting social justice issues to redeem America's soul. *Journal of Educational Administration, 45*(6), 653–671.

Payne, C. M., & Kaba, M. (2007, Spring/Summer). So much reform, so little change: Building-level obstacles to urban school reform. *Social Policy,* 30–37.

Schmoker, M. (1999). *Results: The key to continuous school improvement* (2nd ed.) Alexandria, VA: Association of Supervision & Curriculum Development.

Theoharis, G. (2007). Social justice educational leaders and resistance: Toward a theory of social justice leadership. *Educational Administration Quarterly, 43*(2), 221–258.

Theoharis, G. (2010). Disrupting injustice: Principals narrate the strategies they use to improve their schools and advance social justice. *Teachers College Record, 112*(1), 331–373.

Ullucci, K. (2007). The myths that blind: The role of beliefs in school change. *Journal of Educational Controversy, 2*(1), Article 4.

CHAPTER 5

SCHOOL IMPROVEMENT THROUGH SHARED LEADERSHIP

Julia Kirk

INTRODUCTION

Research has shown that an effective school leader has a school impact of 25% on student gains (Leithwood, Seashore Louis, Anderson, & Wahlstrom, 2004). According to Louis et al. (2010), "leadership is second only to classroom instruction as an influence on student learning" (p. 9). The school principal's role has an indirect impact on student achievement through the principal's instructional leadership with teachers (Goddard, Miller, Larson, Goddard, & Madsen, 2010). The role of the school principal and the complexities of this job have been established throughout the literature (Zepeda, 2007). Furthermore, Leithwood and Montgomery (1982) noted, "Considerable data support the contention that the principal's role is inherently ambiguous and complex" (p. 332). Understanding the magnitude of the school principal role while balancing the day to day activities to focus on what leads to school improvement has become paramount for school leaders (Zepeda, 2007). According to Robinson, Lloyd, and Rowe (2008), "leadership practices are better captured by measures of instructional leadership" (p. 665).

Leadership for School Improvement: Reflection and Renewal
pages 67–83.
Copyright © 2019 by Information Age Publishing
All rights of reproduction in any form reserved.

In the literature on school improvement, as it relates to the role of the school principal, researchers recently have narrowed the focus of studies to one major component necessary for effective school improvement: developing a shared leadership culture to foster teacher leadership. Shared leadership hinges on the school principal's ability to bring about change (Fullan, 2014; Zepeda, 2007), focusing on the improvement of instruction and, therefore, student achievement (Goddard et al., 2010; Marks & Printy, 2003; Robinson et al., 2008; Sebastian, Allensworth, & Huang, 2016), through the development of a culture conducive to shared leadership and an increase in the utilization of teacher leaders (Berry & Farris-Berg, 2016; Katzenmeyer & Moller, 2001; Nappi, 2014). A school principal functioning in the current era of high-stakes accountability should work to form a culture of shared leadership by developing a leadership hierarchy to include teachers as leaders through the development of collaboration, trust, and relationships with teachers.

METHODOLOGY

This chapter focuses on the role of the school principal in establishing a culture of shared leadership to accomplish school improvement. The intent is not to provide a comprehensive literature review of the current research surrounding the role of the school principal in school improvement but rather to focus on research related to developing a culture of shared leadership and growing teacher leaders. Investigation for the literature within this chapter began with an ERIC and Google Scholar search for *principal* and *school improvement* as key search terms, which returned a variety of responses from parent involvement to curriculum development. Additionally, the author of this chapter referenced textbooks and manuscripts specific to the principal's role in school improvement.

After reviewing many articles, books, and literature reviews utilizing the broad *principal* and *school improvement* terms, the author determined that the preponderance of recent work related to the principal's role in school improvement focused on establishing a culture of shared leadership and developing teacher leaders. At this point, a more narrow focus and search related to *teacher leadership* and *school improvement/principal leadership* was conducted to ensure a thorough investigation into the literature. Additionally, a discussion of school culture and change leadership was also found in much of the literature where the focus was on establishing a culture of shared leadership and building teacher leaders.

Therefore, for the purpose of this chapter, only literature related to a culture of shared leadership, including what must occur to create this culture, and teacher leadership were included to narrow the focus yet still provide two key areas for the principal's role in school improvement: shared leadership and teacher leaders. This chapter first is organized by a discussion of shared leadership. Following that, a discussion of the current literature on teacher leadership, stemming from two pivotal literature reviews related to teacher leadership, will be included. Finally, a connection will be made between the principal and the establishment and growth of teacher leaders in a school which leads to school improvement, including what a principal must do to establish a culture of shared leadership and to grow teacher leaders. The purpose of this chapter is to highlight two key strategies for school improvement at the school level: shared leadership and teacher leaders.

ESTABLISHING SHARED LEADERSHIP

A principal cannot improve a school alone (Goddard et al, 2010; Lumpkin, Claxton, & Wilson, 2017; New Leaders, 2015; Zepeda, 2007). Instead, establishing a culture of shared leadership, or de-centralizing the principal role, has been shown as an effective way to handle change (Goddard et al., 2010, Zepeda, 2007). Zepeda (2007) advised that "principals assert their effectiveness by diffusing leadership to a larger set of stakeholders, namely, teachers" (p. 8). According to Lambert (2002), learning and leading are community driven and teachers should take responsibility for not only their own learning, but also leading their colleagues' learning as well, thus creating shared leadership. Lambert's (2002) assumptions for shared leadership include:

- Everyone has the right, responsibility, and ability to be a leader.
- How we define leadership influences how people will participate.
- Educators yearn to be more fully who they are—purposeful, professional human beings. Leadership is an essential aspect of an educator's professional life. (p. 38)

Shared leadership is the key to school improvement (Cosenza, 2015; Goddard et al., 2010; Harris & Muijs, 2004; Marks & Printy, 2003; Nappi, 2014). Wahlstrom and Louis (2008) conducted a national study where they surveyed 4,165 teachers across the United States to determine what factors were most important in both teacher to teacher and teacher to principal relationships that also impacted instructional practices. They found "expanding the decision making arenas in schools to include non-administrators is an important step that leaders can take in long-term efforts to improve instruction" (p. 479). Flood and Angelle (2017) had a similar finding in their study of 443 teachers across 25 schools where they investigated the relationships between trust, collective efficacy, and teacher leadership. Flood and Angelle found that including teachers in a shared leadership and decision making model allowed the principal to include voices of individuals who had the closest proximity to students and therefore the best opportunity to influence school improvement. It is through the establishment of shared leadership that principals can begin the work of school improvement.

TEACHER LEADERS

Moving to a shared leadership environment encourages teachers to rise as leaders among their colleagues. Sebastian et al. (2016) claimed that fostering a strong school climate through teacher leadership is the key to increasing student achievement. Derrington and Angelle (2013) asserted that "teacher leadership matters for school success, not just for the teacher who participates in a leadership role" (p. 6). Sometimes, the principal selects certain teachers to serve as leaders, through involvement on teams or in leadership roles; however, sometimes teachers rise to leadership on their own, through their work in teams, through desire to learn at outside professional development, or other avenues. Wenner and Campbell (2017) noted that teacher leaders were potentially the most influential leader in the school, even more so than the school principal. While the teacher leader is shown to be the most influential leader in a school, teacher leadership is still a structure that many schools are not adopting. For example, Peterson (2016) stated, "At the very heart of our schools lies a potentially powerful resource that often remains untapped—our teacher leaders" (p. i). Danielson (2006) affirmed this by noting, "It is well recognized, but little acted upon, that the greatest professional resource available in every school is the expertise of its teachers" (p. 55).

The following sections examine teacher leadership from the perspective of common definitions of the construct, the roles of teacher leaders, pivotal literature reviews, and teacher leaders as change agents. Additionally, the principal's role in fostering this leadership is then investigated related to building relationships, leadership for change, collaborative culture, and action.

Definitions and Roles

Perhaps one of the reasons why teacher leadership is infrequently used is due to the vague nature of the position or role. Definitions of teacher leadership vary in the literature and "the work of a teacher leader is often undefined, unsupported, and sometimes unrecognized and undervalued" (Killion et al., 2016, p. 4). Definitions vary in specificity, including a simplistic "teacher leaders are (usually) classroom teachers who share their expertise in myriad forms" (Nappi, 2014, p. 2). On the other end of the spectrum, a more comprehensive definition by Katzenmeyer and Moller (2001) is "teachers who are leaders lead within and beyond the classroom, identifying with and contributing to a community of teacher learners and leaders, and they influence others toward improved educational practice" (p. 17). A definition that lends itself more to define the role of the teacher leader to include the principal's use of teacher leaders would encompass both formal leadership roles, which include administrative and pedagogical responsibilities, as well as informal leadership roles, which include more influence on the overall organization in roles such as coaching or mentoring (Angelle & Teague, 2014; Muijs & Harris, 2006). Lovett (2017) gave the most comprehensive definition of teacher leader and teacher leadership found in the literature:

> Teacher leaders are characterized by their enduring commitment to improving students' learning. Their strong sense of moral purpose is what determines their leadership activities. They develop close and collaborative working partnerships with their colleagues through their mutual interest in solving issues of practice that revolve

around helping students learn. Their need for learning is met through recognition that their colleagues are a valuable source of expertise and a sphere of influence to which they themselves contribute. (p. 64)

Wenner and Campbell (2017) noted that the variety of definitions might be due to the differing roles teacher leaders have in different schools. Principals have the discretion to utilize teacher leaders in whatever way makes the most sense for the school, formal or informal, and sometimes a mix of both. One important component to remember, however, when considering teacher leaders is, according to Wilhelm (2010), "leading adults requires a different skill-set than instructing students" (p. 24).

Much of the literature surrounding teacher leadership does not define, purposefully, the actual roles of the teacher leader as they vary greatly from building to building, some formal and some informal. The theoretical role of the teacher leader was captured in definitions above, but in considering how to frame the role of the teacher leader, there is literature to help pave the way. Killion et al. (2016) offered a set of ten assumptions when framing the role of teacher leader:

1. Teacher leadership impacts student and peer performance.
2. Teachers lead, formally or informally, wherever they are.
3. All teachers have opportunities for leadership.
4. Teacher leadership requires that teachers develop capacity for effective leadership.
5. Teachers develop leadership capacity when they are supported.
6. Teacher leadership requires changes in other leaders throughout the system.
7. Teacher leaders take responsibility for their own professional growth and the growth of others.
8. Teacher leadership requires courage, tolerance for ambiguity, and flexibility.
9. Teacher leaders foster collaborative cultures that promote continuous improvement.
10. Teacher leaders collect evidence of impact resulting from their work. (pp. 7–9)

Teacher leadership, then, is by definition both vague and encompassing. The list of assumptions above can assist in the conceptual formation of teacher leader roles. The literature shows that teacher leadership is an important component for school improvement. Delving into the literature further to find the most successful way to go about establishing teacher leaders to foster school improvement serves to expand this component of school reform.

Teacher Leader Pivotal Literature Reviews

Two distinct literature reviews stand as foundational to teacher leadership research; that is York-Barr and Duke (2004) and Wenner and Campbell (2017). Many recent studies cite York-Barr and Duke (2004) as a basis in their discussion and review. Wenner and Campbell (2017) is a newer study but captures much of the more recent literature related to teacher leadership.

York-Barr and Duke. York-Barr and Duke (2004) conducted a review of literature related to teacher leadership, literature from 1980–2004; incorporating 140 research studies. They centered their literature review on the question "What is known about teacher leadership?" (p. 256). York-Barr and Duke found four benefits to practicing the use of teacher leadership for school improvement: "benefits of employee participation; expertise about teaching and learning; acknowledgement, opportunities, and rewards for accomplished teachers; and benefits to students" (p. 258). Since this seminal research review, policies began to emerge related to teacher leadership, interest began to rise by principals and districts to shift their thinking from a principal-centered role to a more distributed leadership style due to the increased demands put upon the administrative positions, states began to incorporate teacher leadership into evaluation for teachers, and universities began to incorporate programs related to teacher leadership certification and licensure.

In 2015, the National Policy Board for Educational Administration (NPBEA) released the Professional Standards for Educational Leaders as an update to the existing Interstate School Leaders Licensure Consortium (ISLLC) standards (NPBEA, 2015). The NPBEA recognized that since the development of the 2008 ISLLC standards, the status and role of educational leaders had changed to include a more distributed style. The revised standards addressed teacher leadership within substandard G of Standard 6—Professional Capacity of School Personnel—which stated that effective leaders should "develop the capacity, opportunities, and support for teacher leadership and leadership from other members of the school community" (NPBEA, 2015, p. 14). Additionally, multiple universities began offering teacher leadership licenses and graduate certification programs (such as Villanova, American, and University of Georgia). Moreover, states utilizing Danielson's (2013) framework for teacher evaluation, such as Kentucky, Illinois, and New York, began to incorporate teacher leadership behaviors into teacher evaluation systems implemented within state education agencies, through the indicator "growing and developing professionally" (Reform Support Network, 2012).

Wenner and Campbell. Additional research that occurred after York-Barr and Duke's 2004 seminal literature review through 2013 was captured in an updated literature review on teacher leadership by Wenner and Campbell (2017). Wenner and Campbell were motivated to conduct this updated literature review for three reasons: 1) teacher leadership was gaining popularity in policy and in university studies, 2) accountability through policy was beginning to shift to include teacher leaders, and 3) teacher attrition was increasing. Wenner and Campbell (2017) found the following themes in the research: "teacher leadership goes beyond the classroom; teacher leaders should support professional learning in their schools; teacher leaders should be involved in policy and/or decision making; and the ultimate goal of teacher leadership is improving student learning and success" (p. 7).

The literature reviewed in the work by Wenner and Campbell (2017) provided continued justification that teacher leadership is an instrumental concept in school improvement. Wenner and Campbell's literature review began with the same notion as York-Barr and Duke (2004) but went into more detail related to specific subject area and investigated equity and social justice as they related to teacher leadership. Themes found by Wenner and Campbell also related to the effects of teacher leadership. They found teachers had "feelings of empowerment for all teachers in a school; colleagues receiving support that is relevant and encourages professional growth and teacher leadership contributing significantly to school change" (p. 10). While a comprehensive literature review has not been completed since 2017, studies that have occurred since the 2013 end point in Wenner and Campbell's review are included in this chapter within their appropriate theme related to teacher leadership.

Teacher Leaders as Change Agents for School Improvement

According to Killion et al. (2016), "teacher leadership is more than another program to be implemented and eventually replaced. It is the transformation of the way educators work within schools every day" (p. 6). Teacher leaders have the ability to change their colleagues' teaching by engaging in leadership practices that effectively communicate and encourage their colleagues. When this type of instructional change occurs, schools improve (Cooper et al., 2016).

Teacher leaders do not have to have established formal roles. Teacher leaders can emerge from their group to lead the group and their colleagues. Through this teacher leadership, all teachers benefit. Flood and Angelle (2017) conducted a study of 443 teachers investigating collective efficacy and trust as they related to teacher leadership and found "the fact that simply working in a collaborative group positively affects teacher leadership demonstrates that leadership extends beyond a formal title or designated role" (p. 95). Teachers, when taking on leadership roles and learning from leaders within their own group, benefit instructionally and collectively, which ultimately benefits the students.

According to Berry and Farris-Berg (2016), not only do teachers within collaborative groups benefit from teacher leadership, but school communities respond favorably to school environments where teachers have the autonomy to make decisions within their classroom and decisions that affect the school as a whole. Within their discussion, Berry and Farris-Berg present the concept of teacher-powered schools where teachers have the autonomy to "collaboratively design and lead many aspects of teaching and learning" (p. 15). In these teacher-powered schools, teachers have decision making power related to instructional materials, professional development, colleague selection, and district assessments. Teachers in these schools also evaluate each other using a peer review model. Teachers in teacher-powered teams "engage in better quality collaboration, focused on more holistic measures of learning rather than just standardized test scores" (p. 16), ultimately raising student achievement. While teacher-powered schools are a specific type of school, the elements of teacher leadership within the teacher-powered school model can be transferred to any type of school and, when doing so, the teachers and school community benefit as a whole.

Berry and Farris-Berg (2016) determined that teacher leadership and decision making was beneficial to the culture of a school, while other researchers focused on the outcome of increasing student achievement, which is a measure of true school improvement. Utilizing Kotter's (2008) eight steps for leading organizational change, Cooper et al. (2016) conducted a case study to examine the leadership practices of teacher leaders who were attempting to make change in their schools. They found that "when teachers work within networks of supportive embedded systems, they can develop and drive change towards an instructional vision that is clear and reinforced" (p. 104). Cooper et al. found five systems that impacted the teacher leadership change process: "personal orientations toward leadership; principal's orientation toward leadership; the leadership team; the school context; and the local context" (p. 104). Cooper et al. (2016), coupled with the work by Killion et al. (2016) and Berry and Farris-Berg (2016), show that teacher leadership creates a culture where all teachers feel successful and supportive while being led by their colleagues, where the school community as a whole feels the decisions by the teachers are valued, and ultimately where a vision for student achievement is clear and student achievement is increased. The previous section has defined teacher leadership and provided examples in the literature to support the necessity of teacher leadership to improve schools. The next section of this chapter focuses on the establishment of a shared leadership culture and teacher leadership through the actions of the school principal.

THE PRINCIPAL'S ROLE IN FOSTERING TEACHER LEADERSHIP

Principals are most effective when they focus on instructional leadership (Marks & Printy, 2003). Yet, instructional leadership is an elusive term (Zepeda, 2007). Research has shown that when principals establish a shared culture and foster teacher leadership, schools improve. Goddard et al. (2010) conducted a study to measure the connections between principals' shared instructional leadership, teacher collaboration, and 3rd grade students' achievement in reading and math. They found a significant effect among all three variables, building upon each other. Additionally, Robinson et al. (2008) conducted a meta-analysis to investigate the impact of types of leadership on student achievement in the existing literature on instructional leadership. They found strong effects related to the promotion and participation in teacher learning and development. "The leadership dimension that is most strongly associated with positive student outcomes is that of promoting and participating in teacher learning and development" (Robinson et al., 2008, p. 667). To further support this point, Sebastian et al. (2016) investigated the connections between principal leadership and student achievement and found the only significant pathway from principal leadership to student achievement was to include teacher leadership: "principal leadership →teacher leadership→learning climate→student achievement growth" (p. 89).

When shared leadership increases in a school, principals and teachers are collectively able to be instructional leaders. When principals combine transformational leadership, build a positive school culture, incorporate participatory decision-making and collaboration, and develop shared leadership, they will be more effective (Marks & Printy, 2003). Yet, establishing a culture of shared leadership and developing teacher leaders is a challenging task. The purpose of this section is to bring to light the processes and actions principals can take to establish a culture of shared leadership and to develop teacher leaders.

Building Relationships

The first step for a principal working toward building a culture of shared leadership is to reflect on the approach to leadership overall and set a positive environment (Katzenmeyer & Moller, 2001). According to Sebastian et al. (2016) "one of the main ways in which principals influence student achievement is through school climate" (p. 90). Leithwood, Harris, and Hopkins (2008) identified influence, motivation, commitment, and the conditions of the school as a strong claim about successful school leadership. A principal's approach to teachers in general speaks to the principal's level of understanding of the value of trust and relationships within the school. To create buy-in from teachers, a school leader must move past the carrot and stick mentality (Fullan, 2014).

To move from a culture of top down leadership to a culture of shared leadership, the principal takes steps toward trust and relationships. Angelle and Teague (2014) noted that "shared leadership is not an output of principal-delegated tasks but is an outcome of collaboration and relationship building" (p. 741). According to Zepeda (2007), shifting to a culture of shared leadership "entails trust, collaboration, support, and advocacy for extending the boundaries of authority beyond the position of the person who holds the title of principal" (p. 8). Sebastian et al. (2016) found that a principal's influence on school climate comes through the purposeful inclusion of teacher voice in decision making. As a principal, understanding one's own relationships with teachers and how one interacts with teachers and supports them can help move a culture to one ready for shared leadership. The first step in this move is trust.

Tschannen-Moran and Hoy (2000) consider trust "a critical factor as we consider school improvement and effectiveness" (p. 585). Trust per Tschannen-Moran and Hoy is not only individual trust, but collective trust, trust of the work group. Trust, then, is a factor to consider between teachers, teachers to principals, and teachers to students or parents. For the organization to be effective, teachers need to be able to trust each other and their leadership. According to Flood and Angelle (2017), teacher's trust in their principal and their colleagues has a great influence on the likelihood and establishment of teacher leadership. When teachers trust each other and their leader, they have the ability to take on more roles and are better ready to learn.

Demir (2015) conducted a study of 378 teachers in Burdur public primary schools to determine the effect of organizational trust on the culture of teacher leadership in primary schools. The framework of organizational trust measured included trust in principals, trust in colleagues, and trust in students. Demir found that teachers' level of trust was an "antecedent of the level of support toward a culture of teacher leadership" (p. 629). Within these findings, trust in administration was actually the highest variable to correlate, meaning a teacher's level of trust of his or her administrator was paramount to the success of a culture of shared leadership.

In order for an organization to be effective, making it ready for school improvement through a culture of shared leadership, trusting relationships must be evident in the school between teachers themselves and between teachers and the principal. "Through teacher leadership, relationships from teacher to teacher can grow stronger as teachers collaborate and learn together" (Flood & Angelle, 2017, p. 86). Principals must love their teachers. This is the first, and arguably most important, secret to change according to Fullan (2011). Loving one's teachers means taking interest in their lives, taking interest in their concerns, and listening to teachers more. Additionally, Wenner and Campbell (2017) found that literature on teacher leaders pointed to relationships, specifically the principal relationships with teachers and teacher leaders. Without supporting and forming positive relationships with and among teachers, none of the areas prime for great improvement will matter because teachers will not have buy in. Teachers trust in principals is influenced by the perceptions of school climate, according to Sebastian et al. (2016).

Once trust and relationships are established, increased collective efficacy will move the school as a whole from one of traditional leadership to one of shared leadership, teacher leadership, and increased student achievement. Angelle and Teague (2014) conducted a study measuring the correlation between teacher collective efficacy, or belief in each other, and level of teacher leadership within their school. They found that the more teacher leadership was present in the leadership hierarchy of the school, the greater the collective efficacy, stating that "teachers who perceive a greater extent of teacher leadership in their school also perceive a greater collective efficacy in their peers" (Angelle & Teague, 2014, p. 746).

Collective efficacy and teacher leadership work together. For example, Angelle and Teague (2014) found teacher leadership fosters collective efficacy and collective efficacy fosters teacher leadership with no indication or prediction of which must come first. Similarly, Killion et al. (2016) stated, "a healthy culture supports and advances teacher leadership, and teacher leadership contributes positively to a healthy culture" (p. 12). From these two studies, it is clear that a positive and trusting culture is both formed by and supportive of teacher leadership. Derrington and Angelle (2013) investigated teacher leadership through the collective efficacy lens and also found a strong relationship between collective efficacy and teacher leadership. "A strong collective efficacy belief among staff is indicative of confidence to achieve the school's educational mission and goals" (Derrington & Angelle, 2013, p. 6).

Once a principal understands his or her own approach to leadership, and has evaluated trust and relationships that exist among teachers and between teachers and the principal, a focus can then be given to the level of comfort to move to a shared leadership model. "The extent of teacher leadership in a school depends largely on a principal's openness to shared leadership" (Flood & Angelle, 2017, p. 86). According to Berry and Farris-Berg (2016) principals should shift from just serving as the sole instructional leader to developing teacher leaders by organizing the school in such a way to most effectively maximize the spread of effective instructional practices, thus creating many instructional leaders within the building.

Nappi (2014) stated that principals must be ready and willing to concede some of their own power in order for the leadership hierarchy to include teacher leaders for this shared leadership dynamic to be effective. To increase improvement in schools, through instruction, principals should empower their teachers (Heck & Hallinger, 2014; Lumpkin et al., 2017; York-Barr & Duke, 2004). Often, however, empowering teachers is a change, a change for the principal and the teachers.

Leadership for Change

Understanding change is necessary for principals (Zepeda, 2007), but it is a process (Hall & Hord, 2006). Zepeda (2007) explained that "it is the principal's role to set forth the conditions necessary for teachers to implement change because change is integral to school improvement processes" (p. 9). According to Kotter (2008), a balance must occur between urgency and focus, movement and reflection; it is the push and the pull leaders must balance to move a system to change.

For change to occur and for the school to improve, learning and growth must take place for students, teachers, *and* the principal. The principal is at the heart of this learning, not only in leading forms of learning, but also in modeling *how* to learn. The terms learning leader or leadership for learning are not entirely new. *Leadership for Learning* was used by Hallinger (2011) and re-emphasized by Heck and Hallinger (2014) and was defined as the incorporation of "teaching and learning focus(ed) on instructional leadership as well as the district and more general capacity-building perspective of transformational leadership" (p. 658). The term *lead learner* coined by DuFour (2002) and re-emphasized by Fullan (2015) takes the concept of ensuring students and teachers are learning one step further.

The term lead learner demonstrates a shift from instructional leader, one leading instruction, to lead learner, one most involved in the learning. Fullan (2015) stated:

> By participating as learners with staff in moving the school ahead, the principal becomes more knowledgeable about problems to be solved and at the same time fosters leadership in others. Leaders developing other leaders at all levels of the system is central to short-term efficacy and longer-term sustainability in systems. (p. 48)

The key to being a lead learner is participation. According to Wilhelm (2010), "a principal who is the lead learner is typically found engaging in professional development side-byside with the teachers, modeling a high degree of engagement and participation" (p. 23). Understanding that change is necessary and becoming the lead learner within the building lays the groundwork to foster shared leadership and develop teacher leaders.

Once consideration of change has occurred and relationships have been established, creating a collaborative culture, a group impact, setting the stage for shared leadership and teacher leaders. Kotter (2008) noted that organizational change requires principals, or any leader, to create a group of powerful leaders who will collaborate and take action to steer change. Teacher leaders should serve as this guiding group if the principal supports their role as leaders and understands self as a leader to interact with this group (Cooper et al., 2016).

Collaborative Culture

If shared leadership is the goal, then a collaborative culture is imperative (Cosenza, 2015; Goddard et al., 2010). According to Goddard et al. (2010), there is a significant correlation between leadership and teacher collaboration and also a significant correlation between collaboration and student achievement. Principals set the tone for their building (Zepeda, 2007). Fullan (2014) argued that principals should spend less time on individual teacher instruction and more time cultivating the group. Fostering a collaborative culture, one where shared leadership has the ability to thrive, allows for more teachers to help each other grow and learn, thus strengthening the overall instructional leadership learning impact of the school. Student achievement improves when teachers have time to collaborate, or plan together, using this time to focus on instructional improvement (Goddard et al., 2010).

A collaborative culture means day-after-day learning is built into purposeful interaction (Fullan, 2015). Teachers work together and are excited about their learning, wanting to do more and better. Harris and Muijs (2004) also discussed the importance of the learning culture, which is established through shared leadership. York-Barr and Duke (2004) found that in culture where there was focus on learning, teachers meet expectations to learn and grow as well as be respected as models. In a collaborative culture steeped in shared leadership, everyone is learning all of the time.

Collaboration is an important part of the shared leadership culture. Cosenza (2015) conducted a qualitative study to examine how teachers defined teacher leadership. The themes that emerged from his study included collaboration, sharing best practices, taking action, role modeling, and formal roles. The most mentioned theme was collaboration, with 14 participants responding that teacher leadership included collaboration. Within this theme, characteristics such as "work with colleagues to improve practice and set common goals; joint decision making to benefit student outcomes, and provide support for one another" were mentioned by participants (p. 87). Additionally, Flood and Angelle (2017) found that teacher leadership truly exemplifies collaborative efforts of individuals who have a common shared goal and work together to reach that goal.

Collaborative culture is an important component to setting the stage for shared leadership, but it is larger than that. Collaborative culture extends the learning and excitement of teaching, increasing teacher confidence and love of learning, to take schools to the next level. According to Fairman and Mackenzie (2015) the natural leadership of teachers in a collegial climate is formed by building trusting relationships and establishing a culture of collaboration. Furthermore, Angelle and Teague (2014) found that teachers' belief in each other, or collective efficacy, increased when more opportunities and teachers perceived a greater extent of teacher leadership was present in the building, which is an indication of a collaborative culture. Additionally, Zepeda (2007) highlights that "people working together for the common good, if nurtured, can yield many positive results—reduced isolation, the generation and refinement of ideas and approaches, and synergy from working with others" (p. 9). Shared leadership can and will thrive when a collaborative culture is established.

The Action of Creating Teacher Leaders

In this chapter, importance of shared leadership and teacher leaders and their impact on school improvement have been reviewed. To set the stage for these two key elements, I have investigated building relationships, leadership for change, and a collaborative culture. The final section of this chapter weaves these constructs together. This section will focus on the principal and the considerations to foster teacher leadership in schools. Derrington and Angelle (2013) pointed out that "principals are critical to teacher leadership support and success in a school. They recognize a job well done, provide empowerment in the form of decision making, and share in the responsibility when initiatives fail" (p. 4).

A principal should consider teachers' needs and desires when developing teacher leaders. Printy and Marks (2006) found that teachers thrived when recognition and appreciation were shared from both the principal and other teachers in the building and when resources were shared equitably and by decision of the collective group, leading to trust among the entire staff. Moreover, teachers in this case study "clarify values, frame problems, set goals, argue respectfully, construct and test theories, reach agreement, and design documents" (Printy & Marks, 2006, p. 127) within their role on the leadership team, creating buy-in and serving as representation for the entire school.

Principals must also provide the physical structure for teacher leadership to work, that is, time and resources. According to Goddard et al. (2010), teachers require administrative support to break through many barriers, some of which are time and structure. Wenner and Campbell (2017) also point out that principals play a large part in creating the space where teacher leaders can do their work. Robinson et al. (2008) found that leaders who created supportive environments, protected teaching time, and set up environments where staff and students felt respected and cared for, made schools more conducive for teaching and learning. While many of these elements may seem small, they are important for teachers and teacher leaders to grow.

While the stage has been set for shared leadership and teacher leadership, there is one additional note found in the literature that is worth discussion in this chapter. Fairman and Mackenzie (2015) actually found that in schools where schools improved through teacher leaders, these teachers often did not refer to themselves as leaders, though they met the definition. Fairman and Mackenzie warned that the term teacher leader might actually be detrimental and instead encouraged fostering the elements of teacher leadership, to include a shared culture, with respect, collaboration, trust, and support to allow teacher leadership to develop informally and naturally without actually labeling or providing formal roles to teacher leaders. Derrington and Angelle (2013) found that principal's selection of teacher leaders was actually negatively correlated with teacher leadership as well and suggested a more informal approach to teacher leadership would be more successful. This should serve as caution in the formality of a leadership hierarchy and encourage principals not to assign teacher leadership roles, but to instead walk through the steps of building relationships, becoming ready for change, and creating a collaborative culture, allowing teacher leaders to rise on their own and find support in their collegial groups, with a principal's support and encouragement. According to Zepeda (2007), "Principals who support teacher leadership opportunities do more than work with groups—they cultivate capacity for leadership among many teachers, who in turn, promote leadership among more teachers" (p. 8).

CONCLUSION

In this chapter, an investigation into the literature surrounding shared leadership and teacher leaders was discussed. Building relationships, becoming a change leader, and fostering a collaborative culture were presented in an effort to set the stage for a culture of shared leadership and to work toward the development of teacher leaders. Teacher leaders both increase the success of the school and also increase collective efficacy of the whole for a positive school culture. The emphasis of the role of the principal was discussed in relation to a lead learner, participating and leading learning for teachers and colleagues, and creating shared leadership. The importance of relationships and emotional intelligence is a theme throughout the literature on shared leadership. Leithwood, Harris, and Hopkins (2008) summarized best by stating that "Almost all successful leaders draw on the same repertoire of basic leadership practices. The ways in which leaders apply these basic leadership practices—not the practices themselves—demonstrate responsiveness to, rather than dictation by, the context in which they work" (p. 27). Therefore, it is not merely about instituting the best practice of shared leadership or teacher leaders, but about the process by which one reflects, refines and adjusts practice to listen more, learn more, and collaborate more.

Researchers have investigated which components lead to school improvement; however, if leaders simply enact these components, without greater regard to the human element of schools, schools will not improve. A strong focus on instructional leadership without the emotional intelligence to interact with teachers and support them will ultimately lead to the downfall of any principal. According to Leithwood et al. (2008) "a small handful of personal traits explains a high proportion of the variation in leadership effectiveness" (p. 28). The school principal has a difficult role. Promoting leadership beyond the principal to include shared leadership through teacher leaders is the key to improving schools.

REFERENCES

Angelle, P., & Teague, G. M. (2014). Teacher leadership and collective efficacy: Teacher perceptions in three US school districts. *Journal of Educational Administration, 52*(6), 738–753.

Berry, B., & Farris-Berg, K. (2016). Leadership for teaching and learning: How teacher-powered schools work and why they matter. *American Educator, 40*(2), 11–17.

Cooper, K. S., Stanulis, R. N., Brondyk, S. K., Hamilton, E. R., Macaluso, M., & Meier, J. A. (2016). The teacher leadership process: Attempting change within embedded systems. *Journal of Educational Change, 17,* 85–113.

Cosenza, M. N. (2015). Defining teacher leadership: Affirming the teacher leader model standards. *Issues in Teacher Education, 24*(2), 79–99.

Danielson, C. (2006). *Teacher leadership that strengthens professional practice.* Alexandria, VA: Association for Supervision and Curriculum Development.

Danielson, C. (2013). The framework for teaching. *Evaluation Instrument. The Danielson Group.* Retrieved from https://www.danielsongroup.org/download/?download=448

Demir, K. (2015). The effect of organizational trust on the culture of teacher leadership in primary schools. *Educational Sciences: Theory & Practice, 15*(3), 621–634.

Derrington, M. L., & Angelle, P. S. (2013). Teacher leadership and collective efficacy: Connections and links. *International Journal of Teacher Leadership, 4*(1), 1–13.

DuFour, R. (2002). The learning-centered principal. *Educational Leadership, 59*(8), 12–15.

Fairman, J. C., & Mackenzie, S. V. (2015). How teacher leaders influence others and understand their leadership. *International Journal of Leadership in Education: Theory and Practice, 18*(5), 61–87.

Flood, L. D., & Angelle, P. S. (2017). Organizational influences of collective efficacy and trust on teacher leadership. *International Studies in Educational Administration, 45*(5), 85–99.

Fullan, M. (2011). *The six secrets of change: What the best leaders do to help their organizations to survive and thrive.* San Francisco, CA: Josey Bass.

Fullan, M. (2014). *The principal: Three keys to maximizing impact.* San Francisco, CA: JoseyBass.

Fullan, M. (2015). *The path to equity: Whole system change.* In A. M Blankstein, P. Noguera, & L. Kelly (Eds.), *Excellence through equity: Five principles of courageous leadership to guide achievement for every student* (pp. 45–54). Thousand Oaks, CA: Corwin.

Goddard, Y. L., Miller, R., Larson, R., Goddard, R., & Madsen, J. (2010). *Connecting principal leadership, teacher collaboration, and student achievement.* Paper presented at the Annual Meeting of the American Educational Research Association, Denver, CO.

Hall, G. E., & Hord, S. M. (2006). *Implementing change: Patterns, principles, and potholes* (18th ed.). Boston, MA: Pearson/Allyn & Bacon Harvard.

Hallinger, P. (2011). Leadership for learning: Lessons from 40 years of empirical research. *Leadership for Learning, 49*(2), 125–142.

Harris, A., & Muijs, D. (2004). *Improving schools through teacher leadership.* New York, NY: McGraw Hill.

Heck, R. H., & Hallinger, P. (2014). Modeling the longitudinal effects of school leadership on teaching and learning. *Journal of Educational Administration, 52*(5), 653–681.

Katzenmeyer, M., & Moller, G. (2001). *Awakening the sleeping giant: Helping teachers develop as leaders.* Thousand Oaks, CA: Corwin Press.

Killion, J., Harrison, C., Colton, A., Bryan, C., Delehant, A., & Cooke, D. (2016). *A systematic approach to elevating teacher leadership.* Oxford, OH: Learning Forward.

Kotter, J. (2008). *A sense of urgency.* Boston, MA: Harvard Business Press.

Lambert, L. (2002). A framework for shared leadership. *Educational Leadership, 59*(8), 3740.

Leithwood, K., Harris, A., & Hopkins, D. (2008). Seven strong claims about successful school leadership. *School Leadership and Management, 28*(1), 27–42.

Leithwood, K., Seashore Louis, K., Anderson, G., & Wahlstrom, K. (2004). *How leadership influences student learning: A review of research for the learning from leadership project.* New York, NY: The Wallace Foundation.

Leithwood, K. A., & Montgomery, D. J. (1982). The role of elementary school principal in program improvement. *Review of Educational Research, 52*(3), 309–339.

Louis, K. S., Leithwood, K., Wahlstrom, K. L., & Anderson S. E. (2010). *Learning from leadership: Investigating the links to improved student learning.* New York, NY: Center for Applied Research and Educational Improvement, University of Minnesota.

Lovett, S. (2017). Teacher leader and teacher leadership: A call for conceptual clarity. Paper presented at *2009–2017 ACER Research Conferences.*

Lumpkin, A., Claxton, H., & Wilson, A. (2017). Key characteristics of teacher leaders in schools. *Administrative Issues Journal: Connecting Education, Practice, and Research, 4*(2), 59–67.

Marks, H. M., & Printy, S. M. (2003). Principal leadership and school performance: An integration of transformational and instructional leadership. *Educational Administration Quarterly, 39*(3), 370–397. DOI: 10.177/0013161X03253412.

Muijs, D., & Harris, A. (2006). Teacher led school improvement: Teacher leadership in the UK. *Teaching and Teacher Education, 22*(8), 961–972.

Nappi, J. S. (2014). The teacher leader: Improving schools by building social capital through shared leadership. *The Delta Kappa Gamma Bulletin, 80*(4), 29–34.

National Policy Board for Educational Administration (2015). *Professional Standards for Educational Leaders 2015*. Reston, VA: Author.

New Leaders. (2015). *Leading from every seat: Empowering principals to cultivate teacher leadership for school improvement.* New York, NY: Author.

Peterson, S. L. (2016). *When the sleeping giant awakes: The lived experiences of teacher leaders and implications for schools and education systems.* (Unpublished doctoral dissertation). University of Southern Queensland, Australia.

Printy, S. M., & Marks, H. M. (2006). Shared leadership for teacher and student learning. *Theory into Practice, 45*(2), 125–132.

Reform Support Network. (2012). *Race to the top at a glance. Evaluations for teacher effectiveness: State requirements for classroom observations*. Retrieved from https://www2.ed.gov/about/inits/ed/implementation-support-unit/tech-assist/evaluations-teacher-effectiveness.pdf

Robinson, V. M. J., Lloyd, C. A., & Rowe, K. J. (2008). The impact of leadership on student outcomes: An analysis of the differential effects of leadership types. *Educational Administration Quarterly, 44*(5), 635–674.

Sebastian, J., Allensworth, E., & Huang, H. (2016). The role of teacher leadership in how principals influence classroom instruction and student learning. *American Journal of Education, 123,* 69–108.

Tschannen-Moran, M., & Hoy, W. K. (2000). A multidisciplinary analysis of the nature, meaning, and measurement of trust. *Review of Educational Research, 70*(4), 547–593.

Wilhelm, T. (2010). Fostering shared leadership. *Leadership, 40*(2), 22–38.

Wahlstrom, K. L., & Louis, K. S. (2008). How teachers experience principal leadership: The roles of professional community, trust, efficacy, and shared responsibility. *Educational Administration Quarterly, 44*(4), 458–495.

Wenner, J. A., & Campbell, T. (2017). The theoretical and empirical basis of teacher leadership: A review of the literature. *Review of Educational Research, 87*(1), 134171.

York-Barr, J., & Duke, K. (2004). What do we know about teacher leadership? Findings from two decades of scholarship. *Review of Educational Research, 74*(3), 255–316.

Zepeda, S. J. (2007). *The principal as instructional leader: A handbook for supervisors.* New York, NY: Taylor & Francis.

CHAPTER 6

DYNAMIC ROLES OF DISTRICT LEADERS IN SCHOOL IMPROVEMENT AND REFORM

Dianne F. Olivier

INTRODUCTION

A critical factor in creating and sustaining school improvement is the level of district support. As school leaders continually work toward school improvement, it is imperative to develop and maintain high levels of effective district leadership. District support directly influences the school's capacity through school level administrators and teacher leadership by focusing on strategies to enhance and sustain effective teaching and learning practices.

Honig's (2012) research stresses identifying "central office staff as key support providers" (p. 733). She posits strong partnerships between central office administrators and school principals offer new and "promising direction for educational leadership" (Honig, 2012, p. 735). The importance and key role of central office administrators are reinforced by the comprehensive national study commissioned by The Wallace Foundation in which "school district central offices fundamentally transformed their work and relationships with schools to support districtwide teaching and learning improvement" (Honig, Copland, Rainey, Lorton, & Newton, 2010, p. iii).

As school systems target reform and improvement across all schools within the district, a significant and beneficial approach to change is indeed "*central office transformation*" (Honig et al., 2010, p. iii). District transformation can result in higher productivity throughout district schools through a re-culturing process within which the district transitions into a *culture of learning*. Honig et al. (2010) outlined a targeted system approach inclusive of essential district characteristics in relation to reform including: (1) focusing centrally on improvement for teaching and learning, (2) engaging the entire central office, and (3) incorporating not only structural changes within the central office, but more importantly transformational strategies for collaboration between central office leaders and school leaders.

This chapter focuses on roles of district personnel and overall responsibilities at the district level regarding districtwide school reform. Varying perspectives and theories of district leadership are considered. The intent of the author is not to provide a comprehensive literature review of district leadership but rather to highlight major district leadership research studies to observe commonalities and to share findings from a recent case study examining intentional behaviors and actions of central office leaders in high-performing school districts. A framework is offered for district leaders focusing on school reform for enhancement of professional and student performance as primary goals in whole district reform and improvement. Overall, this chapter offers educators a view of the essential role of the district in creating a districtwide culture of learning and a framework incorporating district-generated best practices for continual reform and improvement. For the purpose of this chapter, the term district represents superintendent and central office personnel. Terms used interchangeably with district include district leaders, district leadership, central office personnel, central office, or district staff.

INTERPRETATIONS OF DISTRICT OFFICE LEADERSHIP

Perceptions of the quantity and quality of central office efforts toward school improvement range along a broad continuum. Central office personnel share their wideranging responsibilities and the many hats they wear, while school personnel are often perplexed as to the true role of district staff.

Among the varying perspectives of district leadership, researchers cast district leaders as *villains* or *heroes* (Leon, 2008), *institutional actors* (Rorrer, Skrla, & Scheurich (2008), *intermediary agents* (Adams & Miskell, 2016), and *key support providers* (Honig, 2012). While perceptions may differ:

> *district leaders* . . . play a key role in interpreting state-level policy and shaping its implementation . . . create the conditions for teachers and students to succeed in the classroom . . . play an especially important role in the success of reform initiatives . . . are fundamental to reform efforts. (Woulfin, Donaldson, & Gonzales, 2016, p. 117)

KEY FINDINGS FROM RESEARCH REPORTS AND DISTRICT STUDIES

"In recent years, districts have become increasingly accountable for the learning outcomes of students in the schools within the districts" (Cowan, Joyner, & Beckwith, 2012, p. 9). Researchers note that sustainability of school reform is dependent on district support (Appelbaum, 2002) and "districts matter fundamentally to what goes on in schools and classrooms" (McLaughlin & Talbert, 2003, p. 5).

With a renewed focus on district effectiveness, researchers are examining district leadership in relation to school improvement and identifying effective characteristics and practices influencing reform efforts. This section highlights selected research studies and shares findings related to district leadership impact.

Research on school reform has shifted from studies focusing on leadership at the individual school in the improvement process to district effectiveness research (Bedard & Mombourquette, 2015; Gamson & Hodge, 2016; Seashore Louis, Leithwood, Wahlstrom, & Anderson, 2010; Thompson & France, 2015). Researchers have focused on district leaders' supportive relationship with school leaders (Thompson & France, 2015) and have attempted "to identify and understand the roles, practices, and leadership models of effective school districts that find success with the vast majority of their students" (Bowers, 2010, p. 396). Exploration of district reform efforts has resulted in identification of consistent findings: "setting a clear focus on student learning, aligning curriculum and instruction with identified student needs, using data to guide instructional improvement, and providing coherent professional development necessary for teachers to succeed instructionally" (Chrispeels, Burke, Johnson, & Daly, 2008, p. 732). In reviewing these findings, similarities are evident between effective factors for school improvement at the school level and district reform effectiveness, thus, supporting collaboration between school and district leaders in overall school reform.

Leon (2008) challenges the perception of "school district offices, superintendent and school boards . . . cast as 'villains' in the drama of school reform and raising student achievement" (p. 46) and presents research supporting "district leadership as the possible 'hero' in these efforts" (p. 46).

District Leadership Major Research Reports

Leon (2008) summarizes best practices supporting districtwide and school improvement efforts demonstrating significant impact of leadership at the district office. His summative findings center around the *district* as "central office, board of education and the superintendent" (Leon, 2008, p. 46) and "identify leadership behaviors and district actions that provide strong support to schools" (Leon, 2008, p. 46) in the quest to improve achievement and close the achievement gap. The examination of four major research reports on the impact of district leadership and district-level practices provided cumulative evidence that school district leaders can indeed be key players in school reform. Following is a brief overview of district actions from each study addressing the focus question: *"What do high performing districts do to lead and foster a process of improvement?"* (Leon, 2008, p. 49).

Harvard's Public Education Leadership Project Coherence Framework (Leon, 2008) focused on identifying critical elements supporting strategies for district-wide improvement. This coherence framework includes the instructional core or teaching-and-learning process as the central focus supported by organizational elements including culture, structures, systems, resources, and stakeholders, each of which must be addressed by district leaders. This framework also considers the external environment, such as policies, funding, and politics, which may exist outside of district office control, although requiring attention. Each of these critical elements are connected in order to establish coherence resulting in a collaborative district culture, clearly defined structures to address the district mission and goals, alignment of resources supporting district focused initiatives, and consideration of stakeholders (internal and external) for successful implementation of reform efforts.

In a second major study of high-performing school districts, the Springboard Schools (Leon, 2008) identified four systematic differences between high-performing and low-performing districts with high-performing districts including extensive utilization of data in school reform decision-making; provision of ongoing, relevant professional development; establishment of a culture and accountability resulting in balancing centralized and decentralized strategies; and alignment of curriculum, standards, and assessments of student progress resulting in appropriate intervention programs (Leon, 2008). The findings from the Springboard study culminated in the identification of seven additional central office leader roles, along with recommendations for district actions:

> (1) develop and implement strategies to maintain focus and build organizational capacity; (2) invest and use multiple assessments; (3) recruit, manage and develop people and organizational capacity, culture and learning communities; (4) report to the public on all subgroups of achievement; (5) own the challenge of English Language Learners; (6) promote relationship building with unions and the board; and (7) don't get distracted. (Springboard, 2006, as cited in Leon, 2008, p. 51)

Successes identified in the Wallace Foundation's *Leading for Learning* project generated the third comprehensive study report reflecting district supportive actions. Findings from this study validate "central offices are now seen as playing a key role in improving student achievement" (Leon, 2008, p. 52). The two school districts examined in this study re-established the district role in facilitating instructional improvement. The Wallace findings supported strong district leadership in order to generate "large scale improvement across all schools in a district that strong district leadership is needed" (p. 52). The initiatives utilized within these districts focused on consistency in relation to content and teaching methods across all district schools. These districts also sought new opportunities for teachers to learn collaboratively and enhance the use of student data. Several Wallace findings mirror effective practices noted in the Springboard study including use of a common curriculum, consistency in instruction as verified by ongoing preparation and monitoring, and data-driven decision making. Study participants highlighted that "effective schools are greatly enhanced within districts that provide support for the overall instructional program, direction, technical assistance and professional development" (Leon, 2008, p. 53).

The fourth major research report summarized by Leon (2008) was a research meta-analysis conducted by Mid-continent Research for Education and Learning focusing on school district leadership and the superintendent's role. This large-scale review of research on superintendents resulted in four major findings strengthening the critical role of district leadership in overall school reform:

> (1) *District-level leadership matters* . . . when district leaders carry out their leadership responsibilities effectively, student achievement across the district is positively affected; (2) *Effective superintendents focus their effort on creating goaldistricts* . . . . five district-level leadership responsibilities that produce gains in student achievement [include] (a) collaborative goal setting, (b) non-negotiable goals for achievement and instruction, (c) board alignment and support of district goals, (d) monitoring achievement and instructional goals and (e) use of resources to support the goals for instruction and achievement; (3) *Effective districts establish defined autonomy* . . . effective . . . superintendents have set clear, non-negotiable goals for learning and instruction, however, provide school leadership teams with both the responsibility and authority for determining how to meet these goals; (4) *Superintendent tenure is positively correlated with student achievement.* (Waters & Marzano, 2006, as cited in Leon, 2008, p. 54)

These four research studies illustrated positive impacts of district leaders in school improvement and reform. Across the highlighted reports, six major findings regarding central office leadership surfaced:

> (1) the importance of leadership—vision, mission, values and support, (2) the importance of systems alignment and coherence within the district, (3) the need to focus on key priorities and initiatives, (4) the importance of collaborating with people in the organization, (5) the need to make teaching and learning the very core of the district's work, and (6) the achievement of a delicate, but important balance between district and school autonomy. (Leon, 2008, p. 55)

Leon's (2008) analysis of these major findings across the four district leadership studies purports "the research is clear that district leaders can make a positive difference in supporting, empowering and developing scalable excellence across their schools and districts . . . we have the knowledge to achieve what is best for our students and communities" (p. 55).

Districts as Institutional Actors in Educational Reform

Rorrer et al. (2008) acknowledged a void in researching districts as units of systemic education reform. As a result of their research, they proposed "a theory of districts as institutional actors in systemic reform" (Rorrer et al., 2008, p. 307). This theory advanced the evolution of reform which initiated with the first wave as top-down reform, followed by bottom-up reform as a second wave, transitioning to a systemic focus, identified as the third wave (Rorrer et al., 2008). Rorrer et al. (2008) conclude that despite the transition to a systemic focus for school reform, the role of the school district was marginalized with reform efforts centering on inputs from teachers, policy makers, industry, and university level. While many researchers have strongly supported the individual school as the center of reform efforts (Smith & O'Day, 1990, as cited in Rorrer et al., 2008), Rorrer et al. (2008) purport "that districts are vital institutional actors in systemic educational reform . . . as the district as an organized collective is bound by a web of interrelated and interdependent roles, responsibilities, and relationships that facilitate system reform" (p. 308).

Utilizing a narrative synthesis, Rorrer et al. (2008) categorized 20 years of research on district studies and leadership activities in relation to reform into four essential roles of districts in educational reform. Each of these roles were delineated according to the primary activities and processes utilized by the study districts.

Rorrer et al.'s (2008) four essential roles of districts in reform include:

- Providing instructional leadership—evolved as "a collective responsibility of the superintendent and central office administrators" with elements of "generating will to reform and [building] capacity to do so;" (p. 315)
- Reorienting the organization—addressed through elements of "refining and aligning organizational structures and processes" and "changing the district culture," thus supporting systemic reform through alignment with district "beliefs, expectations, and norms;" (p. 318)
- Establishing policy coherence—through "mediating federal, state, and local policy" and "aligning resources" (p. 323) in order to reach identified district goals;
- Maintaining an equity focus—a more recent focus in district reform that must address the attributes of "owning past inequity, including highlighting inequities in system and culture" and "foregrounding equity, including increasing availability and transparency of data." (p. 328)

In Rorrer et al.'s (2008) proposed theory of districts as institutional actors, the pivotal issue becomes understanding and promoting district efforts in relation to reform for the intentional purpose of improving achievement and advancing equity. The term *district* within this theory denotes:

an *organized collective* constituted by the superintendent, the board, the central office-level administration, *and* principals, who collectively serve as a network and critical link to uniting the district and schools in ways to both develop and implement solutions to identified problems. (Rorrer et al., 2008, p. 333)

This systemic reform theory purports the necessity of addressing the four essential roles as interacting relationships in order to ensure an equity focus for improvement achievement is deeply embedded within the district culture.

How Leadership Influences Student Learning

Commissioned by the Wallace Foundation, Leithwood, Seashore Louis, Anderson, and Wahlstrom (2004) reviewed research related to leadership influence on student learning. Part II of the summative report addresses the district's role in educational change and shares successful district policies and strategies for improving student learning. The following district-level strategic actions were among those successfully used to address major systemic challenges within the district and resulted in improved student learning (Note: Each district strategy is detailed in the Wallace Report):

- District-wide sense of efficacy;
- District-wide focuses on student achievement and the quality of instruction;
- Adoption and commitment to district-wide performance standards;
- Development/adoption of district-wide curricula and approaches to instruction;
- Alignment of curriculum, teaching and learning materials and assessments with relevant standards;
- Multi-measure accountability systems and system-wide use of data to inform practice, to hold school and district leaders accountable for results to monitor progress;
- Targeted and phased focuses of improvement;
- Investment in instructional leadership development at the school district levels;
- District-wide job-embedded professional development focuses and supports for teachers;
- District-wide and school-level emphasis on teamwork and professional community;
- New approaches to board-district and in district-school relations; and
- Strategic engagement with state reform policies and resources. (pp. 41–45)

Leithwood et al. (2004) highlight three primary elements for impact on student performance—high quality leaders: *set directions* with clarity of expectations and outcomes and utilize data to assess progress; *develop people* by providing system personnel (administrators and teachers) with necessary and appropriate professional learning and supportive resources in order to successfully reach the intended goals; and by creating a *working organization* that functions to enhance high quality teaching and learning district-wide. Learnings from the Leadership Project support the assumption that "there seems little doubt that both district and school leadership provides a critical bridge between most educational-reform initiatives, and having those reforms make a genuine difference for all students" (Leithwood et al., 2004, p. 14).

Links to Improved Student Learning

A more recent study funded by the Wallace Foundation (Seashore Louis et al., 2010) sought to identify successful educational leadership and link the leadership to improved educational practices and student learning. This six-year study examined the educational leadership effect at both the district and school level. Due to the comprehensive nature of research findings in the final report, specific focus areas of district leadership are highlighted with specific key findings related to intentional district leaders actions briefly shared. [For extensive detail, review the comprehensive final report of research findings.]

Professional efficacy evolved as a major finding from two perspectives: (1) principals' efficacy as a key to district effects on schools and students and (2) how districts build principals' sense of efficacy for school improvement (Seashore Louis et al., 2010). Both self-efficacy and collective efficacy were determine as powerful influences. A few specific study results related to efficacy include:

- Districts that help their principals feel more efficacious about their school improvement work have positive effects on school conditions and student learning. (p. 127)
- Principals who believe they are working collaboratively toward clear and common goals–with district personnel, other principals, and teachers in their schools–are more confident in their leadership. (p. 127)
- Districts contribute most to school leaders' sense of efficacy by ensuring that teachers and administrators have access to worthwhile programs of professional development, aimed at strengthening their capacities to achieve shared purposes. (p. 148)
- Districts contribute most to school leaders' sense of efficacy by emphasizing teamwork and professional community. (p. 148)
- District data-use practices have a substantial influence on principals' data-use practices. (p. 179)
- Higher performing districts tend to be led by district staff who communicate a strong belief in the capacity of teachers and principals to improve the quality of teaching and learning, and in the district's capacity to develop the organizational conditions needed for that to happen (high collective efficacy). (p. 197)

- Higher performing districts tend to be led by district staff who coordinate district support for school improvement across organizational units . . . in relation to district priorities, expectations for professional practice, and a shared understanding of the goals and needs of specific schools. (p. 197)

DISTRICT FRAMEWORK FOR SCHOOL IMPROVEMENT AND REFORM: DISTRICT-WIDE CULTURE OF LEARNING

Collaborative leadership at district, school, and teacher levels is at the heart of scalable, sustainable school improvement and reform efforts. Reeves (2009) described how it is not a single focus on mission and vision that renders the most change (*reform*). Rather, the coupling of this with the school leader's focus on instruction and ability to foster a strong, trusting community among teachers is what creates positive student achievement gains. District leaders are empowered to recognize the need to create structures and develop processes that encourage deeper ownership of district-wide values and professional capacity in order to incentivize proven practices resulting in improved achievement. These deliberate practices by leaders can result in district-wide transformational practices impacting schools throughout the district.

This section highlights a case study of two high-performing school districts in which central office personnel intentionally focused on school improvement and reform efforts by transforming their district into a culture of learning. While varying initiatives (such as content specific efforts, Department of Education mandates, NIET/TAP systems, and professional learning communities) were introduced within each district as reform initiatives, these major findings center on *district leader actions* influencing successful school reform, regardless of the specific initiatives; thus, establishing an infrastructure in which all initiatives are embedded. This infrastructure is illustrated as the *District Leadership Transformational Framework*.

This case study examined the district transformation through qualitative data including observations, document analyses, and individual and focus group interviews. The study participants included central office staff, school level administrators, and teacher leaders from two mid-to-large school districts. The selected districts were recognized as high-performing with the majority of schools labeled as 'A' or 'B' level schools (ratings of A to F), although each district had challenging schools labeled as low-performing (D or F ratings). Intentional focus led district personnel within the two school systems to create and support districtwide learning processes "as an avenue for improved teacher and school performance" (Olivier & Huffman, 2016, p. 305). The actions by district leaders have resulted in continuous improvement at the school level and overall district level. The case study utilized qualitative interviews of central office personnel, school level administrators, and teacher leaders relating to the collaborative learning community process utilized by the districts to create and sustain a districtwide transformational culture of learning. Major findings of the study are offered as a framework

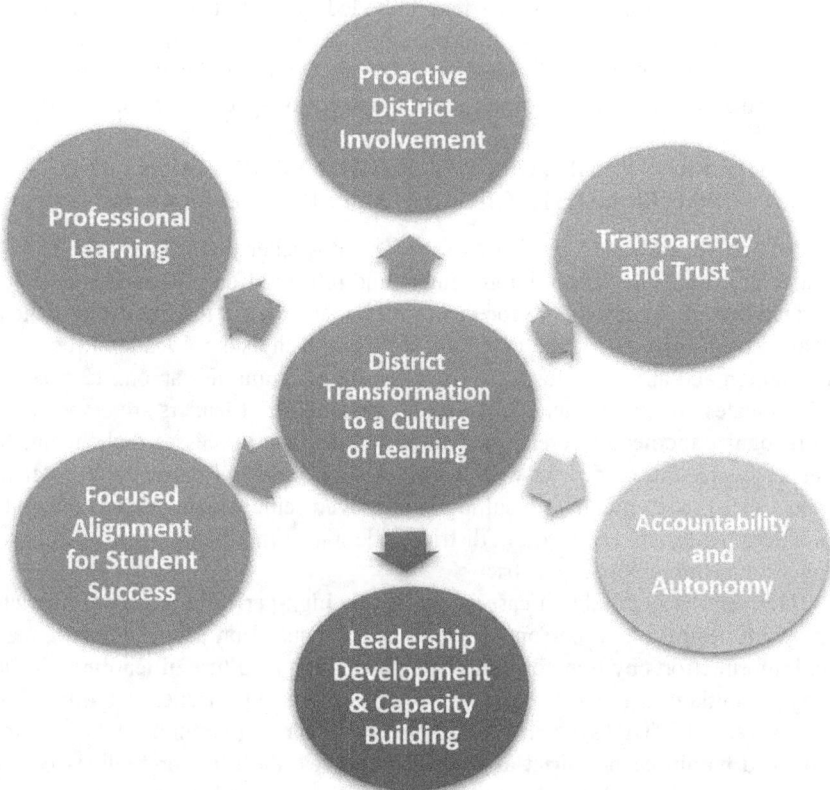

FIGURE 6.1. District leadership transformational framework

for district leaders' *intentions and actions* in collaboration with school leaders (administrators and teachers) toward improved school improvement and reform. District leaders' purposeful actions generated changes in how central office staff collaborated with school leaders for the purpose of transforming to a district-wide culture of learning.

Following is an overview of the study's major findings (Olivier, 2017a,b; Olivier & Huffman, 2015) based on commonalities of district leader practices highlighting the new normal for collaboration between district staff and school staff for successful school improvement and reform.

Proactive District Involvement

Fullan (2005) proposes "Leadership at the school level must be framed in terms of the district's role" (p. 176). District leaders strategically became active participants in the overall learning process and in shaping a district-wide culture to foster high levels of leadership and collaboration throughout the district, across all leadership roles and responsibilities, and beyond school lines. In relation to district staff leading reform efforts, Fullan (2005) stresses that district leaders must clearly conceptualize the reform through an in-depth understanding of the reform content and must actively engage leaders at all levels for the purpose of sustaining improvement efforts.

District leaders created partnerships with school leaders and staff to develop deep understanding of the reform initiatives through collective learning. District leaders consistently modeled shared leadership and vision through continual collaboration with school level leaders as active members of school level collaborative groups focused on collective learning and application of learning. The proactive involvement of district leaders also resulted in greater awareness of school individual needs and thus the ability to provide targeted support and resources to address school identified needs and district inequities. An example of district leaders' proactive involvement in the transformation to a culture of learning within both study districts was the restructuring of monthly district and school administrators meetings. Previously these meetings were administratively focused on policy and procedural issues with delivery of information generating from district leaders and disseminated to school leaders. To support the intended cultural shift, the format and focus of these monthly meetings shifted significantly to reflect "strategically-planned learning opportunities where district leaders and principals and teacher leaders engaged in collaborative dialogue around best practices and next steps...focusing on sustainable district-school reform...framed by strong relationships between the district as a whole and the individual schools in the district" (Olivier, Pujol, Westbrook, & Tuttleton, 2017, p. 131). This shift from previous focus on managerial-administrative matters to instructional leadership and discussions centered on teaching and learning supported the need to embed instructional leadership from both the district and school levels in the districtwide culture (Bedard & Mombourquette, 2015; Honig, 2012).

Transparency and Trust

District leaders were aware of the necessity of establishing a district-wide culture that fosters and sustains transparency and trust among district and school leaders (Hipp & Huffman, 2010; Olivier et al., 2010). "The idea of transparency in leadership also links directly to the concept of organizational leadership trust. If rationale behind decisions is clearly explained to site leaders, it models openness and an opportunity to create a shared theory of action" (Chhuon, Gilkey, Gonzalez, Daly, & Chrispeels, 2008, p. 273).

District efforts for transparency began with a clearly articulated district vision, supported by school-aligned vision. Clarity for the district vision was developed through consistent communication to ensure mutual understanding by all. District leaders articulated high levels of expectations, data-driven decision-making, and communication through common language to remain focused on district-wide priorities. Key district leaders served in a pivotal role as instructional leadership partners and consistently communicated school improvement and reform priorities through collaborative practices around school improvement efforts.

The collaboration and discussion of personal, professional needs among the instructional leadership partners, and the needs of the individual staffs and principals was inherently transparent. This also required a high level of trust since specific needs of leaders, teachers, and students would be openly discussed resulting in the group working to collectively problem solve around the identified needs (Tschannen-Moran, 2009). This framework in which the "districts' visions were clearly articulated and regularly reviewed" (Olivier & Huffman, 2015, p. 11), served as a model for transparency and trust for all leaders district-wide. While transparency and trust was a district-wide goal among all leaders, district leaders were cognizant of the importance of school staff having trust in the central office. Trust in district leaders "is a resource that on the surface seems to be a condition that enables teachers and central administrators to work cooperatively toward shared goals and aims" (Adams & Miskell, 2016, p. 677). The study districts adhered to the goal of transparency from the district level in order to be viewed as trustworthy.

The strong foundation of transparency and trust was also evident through successful data sharing sessions by school leaders and facilitated by district leaders, in which school administrators identified behaviors resulting in improvement (i.e., clear communication, examination of student work, monitoring of progress) and challenges for the purpose of sharing with teachers in order to sustain best teaching practices (Olivier et al., 2017). This shift in analysis and utilization of data aligns with previous studies indicating the necessity to "shift from narrow data gathering to building a widely shared capacity to use an array of evidence to inform the alignment of policy, procedures, structures, programming, and instruction" (Bedard & Mombourquette, 2015, p. 251). Difficult conversations occurred among district and school leaders paving the way for difficult data-driven decisions for school improvement and reform.

Accountability and Autonomy

District leaders adhered to the practice of *defined autonomy* (Marzano & Waters, 2009) and supported school leaders' autonomy in leading reform efforts and school-related initiatives aligned with the district's vision while maintaining accountability for results. While endorsing autonomy, district leaders established non-negotiables promoting a sense of shared responsibility for all staff (district and school-level) and student learning. These non-negotiables set parameters aligned with district goals, such as every school will embed within the school culture a productive process for collaboration.

> The organization of teacher collaboration, the utilization of specific structures, and the interaction between principals and teacher leaders to support teachers, were

all at the total discretion of the principals and their leadership teams. The districts provided resources and models for how this collaboration could be structured and implemented, but school personnel had the autonomy to make decisions as to what would work on their campus. (Olivier et al., 2017, p. 127)

The emphasis on non-negotiables is reinforced by Marzano and Waters (2009) in support for establishing nonnegotiable district goals for student achievement and effective instruction through a collaborative goal-setting process. Additionally, school level progress was consistently monitored by district leaders in consultation with school administrators and teacher leaders to maintain focus on alignment of district and school vision, goals, and objectives.

Leadership Development/Capacity Building

Multiple layers of leadership were used by the district to address district and school level goals. District leaders focused on building leadership capacity throughout the district resulting in development of new leaders, enhancement of knowledge, skills, and expertise of current leaders, and the creation of avenues for individuals to transition from informal to formal leadership positions. District leaders focused on development of leadership capacity among school-level leaders so every school campus shared a vision of learning and collaboration and supportive conditions associated with high productivity of school reform efforts. Through the process of building capacity, teacher-leaders assumed more visible leadership roles and responsibilities (such as, curriculum specialists, master teachers, instructional coaches/facilitators). "The leadership capacity among teachers was critical to sustaining this collaborative, problem solving approach to school and district improvement" (Olivier et al., 2017, p. 126). By establishing more formal leadership succession plans, district leaders were able to sustain a culture of learning as individuals transitioned into formal leadership positions, both at the school and district levels. District leaders continually modeled highly effective leadership practices through interactions with all professional staff and "recognized that strengthening their own leadership capacity, and the leadership capacity in schools, held promise for cultivating rapid and long-term school and district improvement" (Olivier et al., 2017, p. 126). The creation of *leadership academies* by district staff demonstrated strong

> . . . commitment to and investment in, developing leaders with high potential to positively impact the educational experiences of all students . . . [and] . . . serves to develop a talent pool of internal candidates who are actively interested in growing the organization, promoting its success, and are engaged over time to fill formal and informal leadership positions at the school and district-level. (Olivier et al., 2017, p. 132)

The significant restructuring to continual development of current leaders and succession planning by building capacity from within (Honig, 2012; Honig et al., 2010) aligns with previous research supporting "focused and standards-based in-house capacity to support the selection, development, and assessment of incumbent and potential school and district leaders" (Bedard & Mombourquette, 2015, p. 251).

Focused Alignment for Student Success

Both districts consciously focused on the necessity of curriculum, instruction, and assessment alignment to required standards (state and local). Reciprocal relationships existed between district and school goals in order to strengthen alignment. Examination of student work to determine learning and monitoring of instructional practices were clearly communicated by district leaders who allocated resources based on identified needs of each individual school, thus working toward school level success through provision of equitable allocations. District leaders assumed the responsibility to reduce disparity among schools, and accordingly,

> district leaders made the conscious decision to actively engage principals in the same work in which teacher leaders were involved through professional learning, thus developing principals' capacity to re-create this work on their campuses . . . District leaders understood they could not charge principals with this responsibility without helping them develop the skills they needed for success, operating under the principle of reciprocal accountability. (Olivier et al., 2017, p. 124)

Professional Learning

District leaders embedded continuous professional learning for all (central office personnel, school administrators, teacher leaders) within the district-wide culture, modeling best leadership practices and reinforcing collaboration as the norm and an integral part of the culture.

> A community of professional learning developed in the districts from a commitment to continuous learning on the part of all professional staff . . . enabling high quality and focused learning through collaboration . . . and engaging teacher leaders in activities designed to sustain a culture of learning in the district. (Olivier et al., 2017, p. 131)

District support for relevant job-embedded professional learning included the provision of time and allocation of resources to maintain high quality and focused collaboration. With a focus on sustaining school and district improvement, district leaders structured job-embedded professional development to include " . . . teacher leaders sharing best teaching and new learning practices across all schools . . . follow-up and coaching to help teachers implement new learning, and...accountability" (Olivier et al., 2017, p. 126). This priority by district leaders enhanced the ability to scale up school-based practices resulting in the highest student academic outcomes. Learning through collaborative practices has become the process within which the content of all new learning is embedded within the district (Olivier & Huffman, 2015). This positive shift to more job-embedded, intensive professional development required district and school leaders (administrators and teacher leaders), to be present in designing learning-focused PD and to determine success with the application of new knowledge and skills. This more involved, focused process for professional development from within a system is supported by previous research (Seashore Louis et al., 2010).

District Transformation to a Culture of Learning

The six major findings illustrated in Figure 6.1 contributed to the transformation of each district into a district-wide *culture of learning*. Intentional actions initiated by district leaders and supported and adopted by school level administrators and teacher leaders resulted in reculturing the districts with an infrastructure for successfully addressing school reform efforts through strong district-wide collaborative practices.

> District leaders acknowledge that the cultural transformation has created a strong alignment between student goals, teacher goals, school goals, and district goals. This tight alignment, coupled with the balance between professional autonomy and accountability, has provided conditions that are fostering teacher collaboration . . . The intense focus by district....leaders...has resulted in sustainability of effort as evident by the districts' continual growth, increasing levels of student performance, and recognition as...[high] performing districts. (Olivier et al., 2017, p. 136)

In summary, district leaders established non-negotiables while offering *autonomy* and promoting *accountability* through a shared sense of responsibility; district leaders remained *proactive* by actively modeling and participating in the learning process; *professional learning* embedded within the school day became the norm and involved high quality collaboration between district and school personnel; opportunities for *leadership development* and *capacity building* were designed to solidify strong leadership succession; *transparency and trust* were maintained through clear and consistent communication and decision-making; and resources were prioritized to address individual school needs while maintaining *alignment across curriculum, instruction, and assessment*.

This new norm of a strong professional culture fostering ongoing learning for all sustains the high level of commitment to student achievement and improvement as the outcome for all reform practices. The focus on shared responsibilities enhanced a shared commitment for collaboration across the district to support student achievement, school improvement, and overall school and district reform. This research supports clear involvement of district leaders can positively influence school reform and success of students. The intense focus by district, school, and teacher leaders outlined in this case study has resulted in "sustainability of effort as evident by the districts' continual growth, increasing levels of student performance, and recognition as . . . high performing districts (Olivier, 2017a, p. 31).

The case study illustrated district leaders as "key support providers" (Honig, 2012, p. 733) in initiating and supporting systemic reform. The transformation of the central office evolved through the development of strong partnerships between district administrators, school administrators, and teacher leaders. The focus on transparency of actions generated higher levels of trust between district and school leaders, thus enriching the district culture. Rorrer et al.'s (2008) delineation of best practices of successful districts is evident throughout the case study in which the two districts facilitated district-wide reform and improvement, established shared accountability and collective responsibility, adjusted organizational structures for professional learning and leadership development, and aligned resources for student success. Proactive district involvement enhanced the role of central office in district-wide reform efforts and was reflective of strategic actions supported by the Wallace Report (Leithwood et al, 2004; Seashore Louis et al., 2010).

District leaders' intentional and thoughtful actions fostered high levels of professional efficacy as successful collaboration between district and school leaders became the *new normal*.

SUMMARY

This chapter reviewed responsibilities of districts and the critical role district leaders serve in school and district-wide improvement and reform. With resurgence on district effectiveness research, major research reports and district research studies were briefly reviewed with the intent of identifying effective district leadership characteristics and actions. A more recent case study of two high performing districts was showcased to illustrate district-wide school reform success influenced by district leaders' intentional and purposeful actions. Major findings from this case study were offered as a framework for district transformation resulting in a culture of learning. District leaders' actions and collaboration with school leaders (administrators and teachers) were illustrated as district-wide practices generating positive reform results. The intention of the author in highlighting previous research and in sharing study findings is to assist district leaders to be successful in district-wide school reform efforts and to offer a framework for transformation of district leadership. The successes of districts within these studies were supported by intentional and thoughtful actions of district leaders in collaboration with school leaders and staff with the goal of district transformation to a culture of learning. Discussion and findings shared in this chapter affirm previous research adhering to the belief that *districts do indeed matter!*

REFERENCES

Adams, C. M., & Miskell, R. C. (2016). Teacher trust in district administration: A promising line of inquiry. *Educational Administration Quarterly 52*(4), 675–706. DOI: 10.177/0013161X16652202

Appelbaum, D. (2002, February). The need for district support for school reform: What the researchers say. *Research Brief.* Washington, DC: National Clearinghouse for Comprehensive School Reform.

Bedard, G. J., & Mombourquette, C. P. (2015). Conceptualizing Alberta district leadership practices: A cross-case analysis. *Leadership and Policy in Schools, 14*(2), 233–255. DOI: 10:1080/1570063.2014.997936.

Bowers, A. J. (2010). Toward addressing the issues of site selection in district effectiveness research: A two-level hierarchical linear growth model. *Educational Administration Quarterly 46*(3), 395–425.

Chhuon, V., Gilkey, E. M., Gonzalez, M., Daly, A., & Chrispeels, J. H. (2008). The little district that could: The process of building district-school trust. *Educational Administration Quarterly 44*(2), 227–281. DOI: 10.1177/0013161X07311410

Chrispeels, J. H., Burke, P. H., Johnson, P., & Daly, A. J. (2008). Aligning mental models of district and school leadership teams for reform coherence. *Education and Urban Society, 40*(6), 730–750. DOI: 10.1177/0013124508319582.

Cowan, D., Joyner, S., & Beckwith, S. (2012). *Getting serious about the system: A fieldbook for district and school leaders.* Thousand Oaks, CA: Corwin Press.

Fullan, M. (2005). Turnaround leadership. *The Educational Forum, 69,* 174–181.

Gamson, D. A., & Hodge, E. M. (2016). Education research and the shifting landscape of the American school district, 1816–2016. *Review of Research in Education, 40,* 216–249. DOI: 10.3102/0091732X16670323

Hipp, K. K., & Huffman, J. B. (2010). *Demystifying professional learning communities: Leadership at its best.* New York, NY: Rowman & Littlefield Education.

Honig, M. I. (2012). District central office leadership as teaching: How central administrators support principals' development as instructional leaders. *Educational Administration Quarterly 48*(4), 733–774. DOI: 10.1177/001316X1244358

Honig, M. I., Copeland, M. A., Rainey, L., Lorton, J. A., & Newton, M. (2010). *Central office transformation for district-wide teaching and learning improvement.* Seattle, WA: University of Washington: Center for the Study of Teaching and Policy and The Wallace Foundation.

Leon, R. (2008). District office leadership: Hero or villain? *CAPEA Education Leadership and Administration, 20,* 46–56.

Leithwood, K., Seashore Louis, K., Anderson, S., & Wahlstrom, K. (2004). *How leadership influences student learning.* St. Paul: MN: University of Minnesota.

Marzano, R. J., & Waters, T. (2009). *District leadership that works: Striking the right balance.* Bloomington, IN: Solution Tree Press.

McLaughlin, M., & Talbert, J. (2003, September). *Reforming districts: How districts support school reform.* Seattle, WA: Center for the Study of Teaching and Policy, University of Washington.

Olivier, D. F. (2017a). *District support in transitioning from PLC implementation to PLC sustainability.* Paper presented at the Annual Meeting for the University Council for Educational Administration. Denver, Colorado, November 15–19, 2018.

Olivier, D. F. (2017b). *Transitioning from PLC implementation to PLC sustainability: The pivotal role of district support.* Paper presented at the American Education Research Association Annual Meeting. San Antonia, Texas, April 27–May 1, 2017.

Olivier, D. F., & Huffman, J. B. (2015). *The critical role of district support in the development of the professional learning community process in schools: An interactive session.* Conference proceedings of the Annual Conference of the International Congress for School Effectiveness and Improvement, Cincinnati, Ohio, January 2–6, 2015.

Olivier, D. F., & Huffman, J. B. (2016). Professional learning community process in the United States: Conceptualization of the process and district support for schools. *Asia Pacific Journal of Education, 36* (2), 301–317.

Olivier, D. F., Pujol, P., Westbrook, S., & Tuttleton, J. (2017). Transitioning from PLC implementation to PLC sustainability: The pivotal role of district support. In A. Harris, M. Jones, & J. Huffman (Eds.). *Teachers leading educational reform: The power of professional learning communities.* London, UK: Routledge/Taylor & Francis, Inc.

Reeves, D. (2009). *Leading change in your school: How to conquer myths, build commitment, and get results.* Alexandria, VA: Association for Supervision and Curriculum Development.

Rorrer, A. K., Skrla, L., & Scheurich, J. J. (2008). Districts as institutional actors in educational reform. *Educational Administration Quarterly 44*(3), 307–358. DOI: 10.1177/0013161X08318962

Seashore Louis, K., Leithwood, K., Wahlstrom, K., & Anderson, S. (2010). *Learning from leadership: Investigating the links to improved student learning.* Minneapolis, MN: University of Minnesota.

Thompson, E., & France, R. G. (2015). Suburban district leadership does matter. *Journal for Leadership and Instruction, 14*(1), 5–8.

Tschannen-Moran, M. (2009). Fostering teacher professionalism in schools: The role of leadership orientation and trust. *Educational Administration Quarterly, 45*(2), 217–247.

Woulfin, S. L., Donaldson, M. L., & Gonzales, R. (2016). District leaders' framing of educator evaluation policy. *Educational Administration Quarterly, 52*(1), 110–143. DOI: 10.1177/0013161X15616661

CHAPTER 7

UNIVERSITY LEADERSHIP PREPARATION, DISTRICT NEEDS, AND THE IMPORTANCE OF THE UNIVERSITY INTERNSHIP SUPERVISOR IN BRIDGING THE GAP

Jami Royal Berry

INTRODUCTION

The research that exists on leadership preparation programs supports the importance of several core elements in the design and implementation of these programs, including the inclusion of quality internships that both provide comprehensive practice-based experiences and are developed through extensive partnerships with school districts (Cheney & Davis, 2011; Orr, 2011). Additionally, the importance of an experienced practitioner or mentor in facilitating these experiences has been identified as fundamental to the successful implementation of these programs. Despite this, very little research exists highlighting the alignment between the design of the leadership preparation program, the articulated needs of the district, and the importance of the university internship supervisor. This chapter builds upon existing literature to highlight the significance of job embedded leadership preparation, district roles in university partnerships, internships, and the role of the university internship supervisor. This chapter utilizes the Georgia educational leadership certification structure as an example of the implementation of these integrated elements.

JOB EMBEDDED LEADERSHIP PREPARATION

In order to produce graduates who are effectively prepared to lead schools utilizing strong instructional and interpersonal skills, leadership preparation programs must deliberately develop these skills as a part of their curriculum models and must do so through course content that is explicitly linked to job embedded activities (Carlson, 2012; Georgia Professional Standards Commission, 2015). Key educational stakeholders including The U.S. Department of Education, the Eli and Edythe Broad Foundation, the George W. Bush Institute's Alliance to Reform Education Leadership, The Tomas B. Fordham Foundation, the Rainwater Charitable Foundation's Leadership Alliance, and the Wallace Foundation have all outlined similar components necessary vital to effective leadership preparation, including job embedded leadership experiences or internships that take place over time and are connected to course content (Davis, Leon, & Fultz, 2013). Bellamy and Portin (2011) offer that one of the best ways to accomplish this is through scaffolded, job embedded experiences that build in both complexity and rigor and occur over time. These findings have been echoed throughout the literature with both candidates and school districts touting the importance of on-the-job experiences as significantly more important in developing leadership expertise than course content alone without the accompanying internship element (Davis et al., 2013). For instance, in a 2011 study of program graduates, Orr found that having an instructional leadership focus, coupled with fostering high-quality internships, provided new leaders with a stronger sense of self-efficacy and better prepared them to meet the demands of school leadership.

While there is no one-size-fits-all approach to principal preparation, Cheney and Davis (2011) concur that there is an emerging consensus around essential core components. These include experiential, clinical, school-based opportunities that occur through partnerships with school districts where candidates are given authentic opportunities to test their leadership skills in school settings over a significant period of time and while receiving support and feedback from experienced mentors and/or coaches. They further posit that ongoing support in identifying and securing school leadership positions after graduation, as well as ongoing professional development in the induction years, are crucial to success. These types of experiences fulfil the districts' needs of securing leader candidates who are well prepared to lead significant learning improvements while significantly lessening the systemic learning curve of new leaders during their first years on the job.

Although the internship is considered fundamental in providing experiences that enhance core course content and better prepared leaders, concerns with this model include the cost associated with releasing candidates for extended periods of time and the complexities of universities scheduling activities in school systems (Gooden, Bell, Gonzales, & Lippa, 2011). Additionally, the difficulties associated with providing diversified experiences across school types and curriculum areas, as well as universities providing well-versed mentors to help navigate the job embedded context, have all been noted as potential areas of challenge (Duncan, Range, & Scherz, 2011). One way to address these challenges is for universities to have genuine, well-articulated partnerships with school districts that include a discussion of what authentic activities should be included in the internship design, how internship hours can be embedded across the work week, and how universities and K–12 partners can best work together to provide candidates with ongoing support (Gooden et al., 2011). While the features associated with the design of these experiences can be complex, partnerships that are jointly designed and beneficial to universities, school districts, and most importantly candidates, can be foundational to long-term leader success (Burton & Greher, 2007).

DISTRICT ROLES IN UNIVERSITY PARTNERSHIPS

For over twenty years, university principal preparation programs have been criticized by education stakeholders for gaps in course content and for a lack of connection to the daily needs of school leaders. These criticisms have ranged from the general—touting a lack of overall preparation—to the specific—articulating a need for comprehensive, authentic, job embedded experiences (Carlson, 2012). In response, there has been a national push to redesign preparation programs to include job embedded elements, specifically those related to clinical practice that enable graduates to lead change and improve schools. Since preparation programs were introduced in the 1980s, school university partnerships have grown to become increasingly important parts of the overall curricular model in both teacher and leader education (Callahan & Martin, 2007). More importantly, the research has outlined that partnerships between universities and schools must recognize the interdependence and mutual benefits derived from such an alliance in order for it to be both workable for the candidate and valuable to all parties (Lefever-Davis, Johnson, & Pearman, 2007).

In the educational leadership realm, this is especially true because while both the university and the district partners have a shared goal of success for the leadership candidate, the two have distinctly different roles, expectations, and operational bureaucracies. Thus, partnerships that both acknowledge and honor these varied contexts while simultaneously seeking to support candidates are, ultimately, the most advantageous for all parties (Duncan et al., 2011). Considering the contextual elements that impact all parties involved is imperative to creating and sustaining strong, ongoing partnerships (Miller & Hafner, 2008; Orr, 2012). Additional benefits of partnerships between schools and universities include the opportunity to bridge the gap between theory and practice, offer additional formats for programmatic delivery, and keep university faculty updated on the latest trends in K–12 schools (Preis, Grogan, Sherman, & Beaty, 2007).

In considering how best to bridge the gap between theory and practice, the inclusion of partnerships offers various ways to accomplish this goal. First, interacting with K–12 leaders in an ongoing manner can help university faculty stay updated on the latest trends and issues in education (Gooden et al., 2011; Griffin, Taylor, Varner, & White, 2012). While many university faculty members in educational leadership began their careers in the K–12 realm, those who have been in higher education for more than a few years often do not have a clear, updated understanding of the intricacies involved in leading schools in the current accountability-based context (Kearney & Valdez, 2015). This can lead to challenges including a lack of realistic, job-embedded assignments, the sharing of *war stories* as a replacement for providing relevant course content, and basing courses on outdated research and delivery methods. In contrast, ongoing discussion with K–12 partners about both school system needs and how to address them using support structures from both the university and the district as a part of the learning environment can provide a much deeper learning experience and thus, yield better prepared candidates.

A second way that partnerships can help bridge the theory to practice gap by incorporating K–12 school leaders to serve as adjunct instructors at the university level. Utilizing these individuals to supplement the work of university faculty offers benefits to everyone involved. From the university standpoint, having shared roles with K–12 leaders helps the district partners have a better understanding of the systemic structures that exist in higher education. This means that when challenges associated with organizational structures, such as new admissions requirements, do occur, K–12 partners better understand the intricacies of these challenges. From the district standpoint, having their leaders serve in teaching capacities both gives them an insider's understanding of the programs preparing their leaders and offers them the opportunity to have direct input into the improvement work of those programs through course delivery (Lefever-Davis et al., 2007); however, perhaps the greatest benefit of this structure is for the leadership candidate. Utilizing K–12 leaders as faculty members gives program candidates the opportunity to develop strong relationships with mentors who are serving in the exact roles to which they aspire. This relationship moves beyond the content knowledge they share to understanding the intricacies of setting priorities, modeling professionalism, and navigating district frameworks.

When considering programmatic delivery, strong partnerships once again, facilitate better models for this. There was a time when the requirements and demands of a full-time position in the school allowed individuals more time to devote to time on the university campus. The demands of the jobs have grown substantially, and as a result, time has become more limited. Working closely with district partners can have an enormous impact on understanding what models are best designed for candidate needs. For instance, offering classes in hybrid formats that only require students to be on campus for a limited number of meetings, offering classes in school district facilities as opposed to only at the university campus, offering classes on the weekends, and varying class times and meeting dates to mirror the district calendar are all ways that universities can better meet the needs of their leadership candidates. Additionally, when considering the job embedded elements of programs, using faculty members from both the district and the university in the design and support of these experiences can lead to crucial conversations about how candidate gaps might be addressed (Kearney & Valdez, 2015).

Finally, with regard to informing university faculty members on the latest trends in K–12 education, many successful university and school district partnerships include advisory boards with program graduates and other K–12 leaders serving in consultative capacities. These boards assist programs with such elements as input on course design, ideas about job embedded activities, and even the use of retired administrators as mentors for those seeking leadership credentials (Preis, Grogan, Sherman, & Beaty, 2007). While districts have long understood the importance of strategic, authentic partnerships to help them attain their goals (Alvoid & Black, 2014), universities are neophytes in utilizing this model to enhance their programmatic delivery. As this partnership trend at the university level continues, programs will, undoubtedly, continue to grow in the applicability of their work to the needs of districts and leaders.

INTERNSHIPS

School district and university relationships that include job embedded elements and internships for candidates are among the most fruitful partnerships (Stevenson & Shetley, 2015), and this is true at both the teacher and leader levels. While the two experiences are well aligned in purpose, the design differs based on the students served because the majority of individuals undergoing teacher internships are full time students while the bulk of those in leadership programs are full time educators. The challenges associated with the design and implementation of these internships can be mitigated through authentic district partnerships and strong university mentors.

Teacher Internships

Student teaching or the teacher internship is viewed as the most important aspect of the teacher preparation program because of the opportunity it provides for prospective teachers to gain on-the-job insight into the work of the teacher (Kent, 2001). Perhaps the most important aspect of the internship program in teacher education is that it ensures a comprehensive, professional preparation of prospective teachers. Offering the opportunity to integrate theory and practice, plan and deliver lessons properly, critically analyze their own and peers' teaching styles, and improve themselves in the light of feedback given by supervisors (Parveen &

Mirza, 2012), the internship is considered by many to be the most fundamental aspect of teacher education because through it, candidates truly begin to understand the scope of the profession. Many teacher preparation programs concentrate their efforts on providing quality opportunities during the internship experience to better prepare teacher candidates with both pedagogical expertise and the skills necessary to help them teach diverse students. In fact, many institutions have added curricular elements that help teacher education candidates better understand the systemic disparities that exist in communities and to use this information to help them craft more culturally relevant lessons (Simons et al., 2012). Including these pieces in the overall delivery model has been shown to generate better prepared educators who stay in the profession over the long haul (McKinney, Haberman, Stafford-Johnson, & Robinson, 2008).

When considering the design of the student teaching experience, crucial aspects are that the work is job embedded and includes learning that is situated in the context of practice and supported by mentor colleagues (Ross et al., 2011). Historically, these experiences have come at the end of programs of study, often as the capstone activity during the final semester; however, there has been a trend in recent years to put individuals into the field for *mini* internships at earlier points in their programs. Doing so offers the opportunity to learn and apply new pedagogical strategies throughout the program of study, thus enabling knowledge acquisition and application simultaneously (McKinney et al., 2008). Of equal importance, these earlier internships give prospective teachers a clearer understanding of the context of the job while they are still taking coursework. This strategy leads to a stronger foundation of preparation that is based upon a comprehensive, longitudinal accumulation of professional expertise that bears increased pedagogical understanding and stronger self-efficacy for novice teachers (Hunzicker, 2012).

One of the major challenges of the teacher internship from the university standpoint is with regard to the supervision element of the work. Often, the task of supervising falls on junior faculty, adjunct faculty, or retired teachers who have little or outdated knowledge of the intricacies of the current educational context (Kent, 2001). Additionally, colleges of education are notoriously slow to change systems and procedures once they are established (Rodgers & Keil, 2007). This structure can mean that the internship varies greatly with regard to the quality of mentorship and guidance. One of the best models to address this challenge is the use of a cooperative learning triad that includes the teacher candidate, the cooperating classroom teacher, and the university supervisor meeting regularly to articulate expectations and understandings (Steadman & Brown, 2011). When these triad relationships are well matched and guided by an environment of support, candidates benefit from the real-world understandings of the cooperating teacher, the research-based recommendations of the university professor, and the integrated, real-time feedback of the two in tandem. A study by Petti (2013) found that both principals and candidates felt that this structure enhanced candidates' professional development and classroom skills.

In considering how teacher internships relate to leadership internships, the purpose of the two are similar, but the design and accompanying challenges have marked contextual differences. Nevertheless, studies show that school district/university partnerships focused on creating internship programs at both levels with committed university mentors, cooperating teachers or mentor leaders within the school, and ongoing candidate support meetings with both individuals simultaneously resulted in the strongest university/district partnerships and experiences for students (Elliott, Isaacs, & Chugani, 2010).

Educational Leadership Internships

In considering the rationale, design, and challenges of the educational leadership internship, there are strong similarities as well as marked dissimilarities between these experiences and those of aspiring teachers. First, with regard to purpose, educational leadership internships give candidates an opportunity to view systems and practices through a global lens that differs dramatically from the lens of the classroom teacher (Sappington, Baker, Gardner, & Pacha, 2010), and job embedded experiences serve as the vehicle for leadership candidates to gain real world knowledge through authentic on-the-job experiences. In fact, Orr (2012) found quality internships had a positive relationship to how principals viewed their jobs as well as their engagement over the course of time. Additionally, these experiences can help prospective leaders gain a clear understanding of the expectations of the role. Brown-Ferrigno (2003) referenced this shift as a transformation that is necessary to the successful transition from the teacher role to that of a school leader. These findings are similar to those in the teacher internship literature that found that introducing teacher candidates to internship experiences and strong mentors throughout their teacher training is imperative to building a successful career foundation (Parveen & Mirza, 2012).

In contrast to teacher internships, however, one discernible distinction with leadership internships is that most frequently leadership candidates are simultaneously employed as fulltime teachers within schools. This shift means that while the purpose of the internship, to supply opportunities for real world application, is similar, the design varies dramatically from the teacher level to the leadership level. In educational leadership programs, one frequently utilized model includes the majority of the candidate's job embedded experiences taking place at the location where he or she teaches in the district (Valle, Almager, Molina, & Claudet, 2015). Nevertheless, programs and even national accrediting bodies have made steps to enhance this structure, including requirements that candidates have varied experiences working with diverse student populations and across school levels and types. Adding this element to the conditions aids in providing candidates richer experiences because the previous design meant that candidates were really tied to the quality of their mentors in a single school to determine the overall worth of the internship experience. While this is still a factor, it is lessened by the requirement that candidates have varied experiences across school settings. As was the case in the teacher internship model, another way to mitigate this challenge is through the use of a candidate support team. This support team includes not only the primary site-based mentor, but also a university mentor, and in some cases an additional individual who serves as a liaison between the two known as a leadership coach (Georgia Professional Standards Commission, 2015; *University of Georgia Educational Leadership Program Handbook*, 2017).

Another challenge with the design of the leadership internship is with regard to the ability to attain a critical mass of authentic experiences while simultaneously working fulltime. Many educational leadership programs have gone to a model whereby candidates are required to complete a certain number of job embedded activities as a part of each course taken in the preparation program. Additionally, some states have added internship requirements like explicitly tying activities to state and national standards, requiring a minimum number of hours of job embedded performances across semester and/or the program overall, and performance-based exit exams that include ongoing application of knowledge and are decoupled from the university course requirements. Finally, some states have shifted to a tiered certification model in which initial leadership candidates are required to gain one level of internship hours, and advanced leadership candidates are required to gain a higher number of hours, with the requirements increasing in both time and intricacy as candidates matriculate to the next level (Georgia Professional Standards Commission, 2015; *University of Georgia Educational Leadership Program Handbook,* 2017). This shift, frequently accompanied by an articulated requirement that initial preparation is more closely tied to content knowledge, allows individuals pursuing initial leadership certification to *dip their toes* in the leadership realm while still teaching. A second benefit of this model, is that it enables leadership candidates to have truly scaffolded experiences that build in both scope and complexity over the course of multiple programs of study. Research shows that programs that align coursework and assignments aimed at stronger instructional and cultural practice with internship experiences, and are facilitated by comprehensive university supervision, benefit leader candidates and ultimately, schools (Perez, Uline, Johnson, James-Ward, & Basom, 2011).

UNIVERSITY INTERNSHIP SUPERVISOR

As highlighted previously in this chapter, the supervision of internships for both teacher and leadership preparation candidates is imperative. In both areas, university supervisors play a crucial role in bridging the gap between the institution of higher education and the K–12 context (Griffin et al., 2012; Kearney & Valdez, 2015; Kent, 2001). Thus, the most effective supervisors are those who have a clear understanding of both. While frequently individuals serving in these roles have retired from the K–12 context, this in and of itself is not enough to ensure appropriate supervision for candidates. Universities must continue to work to put structures in place to assure that the supervision provided is both timely and comprehensive for candidates. Resources such as program handbooks that are created using multiple stakeholder voices and expertise, training for individuals serving as candidate coaches and mentors, and participation in university sponsored professional development activities are but a few ways to accomplish this. Additionally, it is imperative that the university supervisor participates in ongoing meetings with the leadership candidate, the K–12 mentor, and the university faculty members. Given the complex structures already in place at the university level, there are models available for replication, and clearly articulated internship structures should become part of the ongoing functioning of educational leadership programs.

According to Coleman (2016), one of the great challenges at the university level is tied to the lack of sufficient faculty required for the adequate function of programs. One area of major concern is that programs are typically staffed utilizing an understanding of university structures related to course load and size as opposed to a deeper knowledge of the requirements associated with supervising educational leadership candidates under the new constructs required by states and on the national level. Resultantly, the need for comprehensive course redesign to include a limited number of candidates on each supervisor's load, and course release for university supervisors who are required to be in schools, is crucial. Looking to the teacher internships supervision structures for examples of how to accomplish this is one good first step in both creating workable structures to support candidates and in simultaneously offering to institutions of higher education a concrete way to rethink course loads and structures.

Further, if institutions are going to hire part-time instructors to serve as educational leadership internship supervisors, an understanding of these individuals' current content knowledge is vital. Beyond simply being former school leaders, effective internship supervisors must have current knowledge of the trends and requirements of the positions to which their candidates aspire, and authentic relationships with the school systems in which they are supervising candidates. Internship supervisors should help develop and participate in training activities for candidates, and have updated knowledge in instructional and cultural elements imperative to leadership success (Griffin et al., 2012). With regard to content knowledge, just as current teachers and leaders are required to participate in ongoing, job embedded professional development, universities should put in place similar requirements for the supervisors they are placing in schools. These professional development activities can be offered through school systems, the universities themselves, state and national organizations, or through a combination of these venues.

Having active relationships with school districts is, again, an essential component of the success of university supervisors in supporting the work of the educational leadership candidate. These relationships must include ongoing on-site supervision and mentoring, observations of the candidate within the school setting, and face to face or synchronous virtual meetings that give the candidate, the university professor, the internship supervisor, and the site based mentor the opportunity to discuss expectations, school and candidate needs, and the candidate's performance in real time. Assuring that these elements are in place, helps to ensure that candidates will have the most successful experiences. Additionally, this structure is extraordinarily beneficial to those at the university level because utilizing supervisors who meet these criteria will help universities stay cognizant in the K–12 context and provides opportunities for the continued growth and development of the candidate, the supervisor, the university faculty, and the relationship between the institution and the district (Valle et al., 2015).

THE GEORGIA MODEL

Multiple challenges with traditional leadership preparation programs have been identified, and universities, K–12 districts, states, and even national groups have worked to address these areas of need through both policy and practice (Barnes, 2015). To this end, the State of Georgia has redesigned its educational leadership certification structure to include articulated internship requirements at both the Tier I (assistant principal) and Tier II (principal) levels. As a part of this national shift, Georgia's redesigned model takes elements from the teacher internship model including the required component of university/district partnerships and a university provided internship supervisor, in an effort to provide candidates with the strongest possible job embedded experience. Creating an internship component that allows candidates to practice hands-on, applicable leadership skills within diverse school settings facilitates a demonstration of individual leadership abilities and offers both university faculty members and district partners to support candidates throughout the learning process (Reel, 2009).

Georgia's supervised residency model provides candidates opportunities to practice and demonstrate proficiency in leadership tasks and skills that, when coupled with quality, engaging, and professionally valuable coursework, prepares them to be effective educational leaders. At the Tier I level, these experiences include a minimum of 250 hours of job embedded work, and at the Tier II level, a minimum of 750 hours is required (Georgia Professional Standards Commission, 2015). Candidates are supported throughout their internship experiences at both levels by the Beginning Leader Support Team (BLST), a group comprised of university faculty, a university supervisor, and a school mentor. The university supervisor is the candidate's main support through this process and is the point of entry to discussions with each candidate's school mentor through the mechanism of the BLST.

Both levels of residency experiences provide candidates with substantial responsibilities for leading, facilitating, and making decisions typical of educational leaders that involve direct interaction and involvement with appropriate staff, students, parents, and community leaders. Individual leader residency plans focus on the candidates' performance needs specific to their respective school and/or school districts and on growth measures related to each standard and element. In this manner, the candidates achieve a degree of praxis, or theory-in-action, as they reflect upon their classroom-based instruction in real-time and in real world contexts (*University of Georgia Educational Leadership Program Handbook*, 2017).

Successful completion of each semester of supervised educational leadership residency, as determined by university internship supervisor and school personnel, is required for enrollment in each successive semester of supervised residency. When all three semesters are completed, the candidate has completed the performance-based certification core of the degree program. The supervised residency is tailored to support candidates in mastering knowledge, understanding, and application of both state and national standards. Candidates are required to engage in work across all state leadership standards and elements and are required to do so across multiple school types and levels in order to assure a comprehensive residency experience (*University of Georgia Educational Leadership Program Handbook*, 2017).

RECOMMENDATIONS

This chapter has highlighted the importance of several major areas necessary to the successful preparation of school leaders including strong university/district partnerships, university supervisors with a commitment to continuous improvement, and robust, scaffolded internship structures. With regard to university/district partnerships, facilitating these through ongoing conversation about how best to bridge the gap between theory and practice is imperative to candidate success (Gooden et al., 2011). Additionally, these relationships bring value to districts by helping to keep stakeholders updated on the context of the universities preparing their candidates and to universities by giving them an opportunity to stay current in the K–12 context. University supervisors with a commitment to continuous improvement, are fundamental both because of how these individuals approach their work with candidates and in how they conceptualize their own continued growth and development. Hiring former K–12 leaders to serve in these roles is a good first step, but this experience must be supplemented with current knowledge of the trends and requirements of the positions to which their candidates aspire. Because of the constantly changing constructs of school leadership, this ongoing growth is imperative to the successful support of candidates. Lastly, in considering how to best structure internships for educational leadership candidates, the scaffolded model, a design where experiences build in complexity and scope over time, where initial programmatic work is based on the acquisition of content knowledge, and where subsequent experiences build from this understanding, is recommended as the strongest foundation for aspiring leaders. Building these structures within authentic university/district partnerships that are supported by supervisors who constantly seek and share new expertise is one of the best possible ways to align programmatic content and delivery with the complex and ever-changing needs of school leaders.

REFERENCES

Alvoid, L., & Black, W. L., Jr. (2014). The changing role of the principal: How high-achieving districts are recalibrating school leadership. *Center for American Progress*. Retrieved from https://www.americanprogress.org/issues/education-K–12/reports/2014/07/01/93015/the-changing-role-of-the-principal/

Barnes, F. D. (2015). *Principal professional development: A multiple case exploratory study of district-led aspiring principal programs through the lens of knowledge management*. Unpublished doctoral dissertation, Harvard University, Boston, MA.

Bellamy, G., & Portin, B. (2011). *Toward district-operated, academically supported principal preparation: The leadership pathways design*. Presentation, Pittsburgh, PA: Convention of the University Council of Educational Administration.

Brown-Ferrigno, T. (2003). Becoming a principal: Role conception, initial socialization, roleidentity transformation, purposeful engagement. *Educational Administration Quarterly, 39*(4), 468–503.

Burton, S. L., & Greher, G. R. (2007). School-university partnerships: What do we know and why do they matter? *Arts Education Policy Review, 109*(1), 13–24.

Callahan, J. L., & Martin, D. (2007). The spectrum of school–university partnerships: A typology of organizational learning systems. *Teaching and Teacher Education, 23*(2), 136–145.

Carlson, C. B. (2012). From partnership formation to collaboration: Developing a state mandated university-multidistrict partnership to design a PK–12 principal preparation program in a rural service area. *Planning and Changing, 43*(3/4), 363.

Cheney, G. R., & Davis, J. (2011). Gateways to the principalship: State power to improve the quality of school leaders. *Center for American Progress*. Retrieved from https://www.americanprogress.org/issues/education-K–12/reports/2011/10/24/10461/gateways-to-the-principalship/

Coleman, L. B. (2016). *University educational leadership program coordinators' perceptions of university-school district partnership development*. Unpublished doctoral dissertation, Auburn University, Auburn, AL.

Davis, S. H., Leon, R. J., & Fultz, M. (2013). How principals learn to lead: The comparative influence of on-the-job experiences, administrator credential programs, and the ISLLC standards in the development of leadership expertise among urban public school principals. *International Journal of Educational Leadership Preparation, 8*(1), 1.

Duncan, H., Range, B., & Scherz, S. (2011). From professional preparation to on-the-job development: What do beginning principals need? *International Journal of Educational Leadership Preparation, 6*(3), 3.

Elliott, E. M., Isaacs, M. L., & Chugani, C. D. (2010). Promoting self-efficacy in early career teachers: A principal's guide for differentiated mentoring and supervision. *Florida Journal of Educational Administration & Policy, 4*(1), 131–146.

Georgia Professional Standards Commission. (2015). *Georgia professional standards commission educational leadership program guidelines*. Atlanta, GA: Georgia Professional Standards Commission State Office.

Gooden, M. A., Bell, C. M., Gonzales, R. M., & Lippa, A. P. (2011). Planning university-urban district partnerships: Implications for principal preparation programs. *Educational Planning, 20*(2), 1–13.

Griffin, L. L., Taylor, T. R., Varner, L. W., & White, C. L. (2012). Staying the course: A model leadership preparation program that goes the distance. *Planning and Changing, 43*(1/2), 57.

Hunzicker, J. (2012). Professional development and job-embedded collaboration: How teachers learn to exercise leadership. *Professional development in education, 38*(2), 267–289.

Kearney, W. S., & Valadez, A. (2015). Ready from day one: An examination of one principal preparation program's redesign in collaboration with local school districts. *Educational Leadership and Administration, 26*, 27.

Kent, S. (2001). Supervision of student teachers: Practices of cooperating teachers prepared in a clinical supervision course. *Journal of Curriculum and Supervision, 16*(3), 228–244.

Lefever-Davis, S., Johnson, C., & Pearman, C. (2007). Two sides of a partnership: Egalitarianism and empowerment in school-university partnerships. *The Journal of Educational Research, 100*(4), 204–210.

McKinney, S. E., Haberman, M., Stafford-Johnson, D., & Robinson, J. (2008). Developing teachers for high-poverty schools: The role of the internship experience. *Urban Education, 43*(1), 68–82.

Miller, P. M., & Hafner, M. M. (2008). Moving toward dialogical collaboration: A critical examination of a university-school-community partnership. *Educational Administration Quarterly, 44*(1), 66–110.

Orr, M. T. (2011). Pipeline to preparation to advancement: Graduates' experiences in, through, and beyond leadership preparation. *Educational Administration Quarterly, 47*(1), 114–172.

Orr, M. T. (2012). When districts drive leadership preparation partnerships: Lessons from six urban district initiatives. *Best Practice, 9*(3), 3–17.

Parveen, S., & Mirza, N. (2012). Internship program in education: Effectiveness, problems and prospects. *International Journal of Learning and Development, 2*(1), 487–498.

Perez, L. G., Uline, C. L., Johnson, J. F., Jr., James-Ward, C., & Basom, M. R. (2011). Foregrounding fieldwork in leadership preparation: The transformative capacity of authentic inquiry. *Educational Administration Quarterly, 47*(1), 217–257.

Petti, A. D. (2013). Seeking mutual benefit: University and districts as partners in preparation. *School-University Partnerships: The Journal of the National Association for Professional Development Schools, 6*(2), 32–48.

Preis, S., Grogan, M., Sherman, W. H., & Beaty, D. M. (2007). What the literature say about the delivery of educational leadership programs in the United States. *Journal of Research on Leadership Education, 2*(2), 1–36.

Reel, T. B. (2009). *Program evaluation: The effects of a district-led leadership preparation program on aspiring school leaders.* Doctoral dissertation, Gardner-Webb University, Boiling Springs, NC. Retrieved from https://core.ac.uk/download/pdf/53025894.pdf

Rodgers, A., & Keil, V. L. (2007). Restructuring a traditional student teacher supervision model: Fostering enhanced professional development and mentoring within a professional development school context. *Teaching and Teacher Education, 23*(1), 63–80.

Ross, D., Adams, A., Bondy, E., Dana, N., Dodman, S., & Swain, C. (2011). Preparing teacher leaders: Perceptions of the impact of a cohort-based, job embedded, blended teacher leadership program. *Teaching and Teacher Education, 27*(8), 1213–1222.

Sappington, N., Baker, P. J., Gardner, D., & Pacha, J. (2010). A signature pedagogy for leadership education: Preparing principals through participatory action research. *Planning and Changing, 41*(3/4), 249.

Simons, L., Fehr, L., Blank, N., Connell, H., Georganas, D., Fernandez, D., & Peterson, V. (2012). Lessons learned from experiential learning: What do students learn from a practicum/internship? *International Journal of Teaching and Learning in Higher Education, 24*(3), 325–334.

Steadman, S. C., & Brown, S. D. (2011). Defining the job of university supervisor: A department-wide study of university supervisors' practices. *Issues in Teacher Education, 20*(1), 51.

Stevenson, Z., & Shetley, P.R. (2015). School district and university leadership development collaborations: How do three partnerships line up with best practices? *Journal for Students Placed at Risk, 20*(1–2), 169–181.

University of Georgia Educational Leadership Program Handbook. (2017). Athens, GA: University of Georgia.

Valle, F., Almager, I. L., Molina, R., & Claudet, J. (2015). Answering the call for 21st century instructional leadership: A case study of a school district and university job-embedded aspiring leaders partnership. *Open Journal of Leadership, 4*(03), 86.

CHAPTER 8

SCHOOL LEADERSHIP RENEWAL

Cherie Barnett Gaines

INTRODUCTION

School improvement for student success necessitates that students, teachers, school and district leaders, higher education institutes, parents, and the community must work together to blend what is *required* and what is *best*. Teachers and leaders must have support through training and resources to be successful in the development of essential school factors such as quality instruction, curriculum development, personalized learning environments for students, professional learning opportunities for educators, learning-centered leadership, links to the school community, and monitoring of progress in the schools (Murphy, 2013). Each of these has been discussed in the chapters of this book. Planning for school improvement requires educators to be knowledgeable of the policies and processes for school improvement as well as the recent trends in school improvement research.

Gaines (Chapter 1), Lomascolo (Chapter 2), Koerber and Ritchie (Chapter 3), and Martinez (Chapter 4) reviewed legislation and reports such as the Elementary and Secondary Education Act (ESEA); the Equality of Educational Opportunity Study, also known as the Coleman Report; the Jencks Report; *A Nation at Risk*; Goals 2000; No Child Left Behind (NCLB); Race to the Top; School Improvement Grants; and the Every Students Succeeds Act. These seminal education legislations scaffold, affirming the nation's commitment to educational accountability and providing equal opportunities for students, especially those who are considered our nation's most at risk of failure—those marginalized students—including students of color, students with disabilities, LGBTQ students, and students with differing religious and national origins (Coleman, 1966; ESEA, 1965). These reviews also examined in-school factors, such as curriculum content, standards and expectations of students, time devoted to education, teacher quality, and educational leadership as well as out-of-school factors, including family environments and socioeconomic status of students and how all of these affect student performance (Jencks & Brown, 1975; Superfine, 2005; United States Department of Education [USDOE], 2008). As the authors begin to examine standards-based curriculum and accountability measures based on those standards, the essential nature of school context becomes apparent to achieve ever-increasing academic goals (Superfine, 2005). Continuing to draw from the literature, authors discussed the implications of federal policy on education at the state level and examined the trends of the school improvement movement, focusing on meaningful assessment, leadership preparation, and shared leadership.

As volume contributors identify in subsequent chapters, leadership in schools is crucial to effective school improvement. Understanding the principal's role in creating a climate of shared leadership is essential to creating efficacy in teachers and teacher success in the classroom. As the school principal's role has shifted from managerial to instructional leadership, teachers, parents, and students look to the principal for guidance in creating a shared climate, where all stakeholders feel involved, realizing their own roles in fostering school improvement. Through shared leadership, in both formal and informal roles, teachers strengthen instructional practices which, in turn, improves student achievement, creating a positive culture for all. Supporting principals as they work toward school improvement, district leaders directly influence the school's capacity through collaboration, focusing on principal and teacher empowerment. Kirk's chapter discusses school culture from the principal's perspective, leading to the following chapter where Olivier reinforces this aspect from the district level, proposing that relationships increase efficacy of all educational stakeholders. Berry continues building on this theme of relationship building by addressing the partnership that is needed as teachers and school leaders are trained at the university level, and continuing these relationships as school leaders become functional in their own schools. The following sections offer some lessons learned from the chapters in this volume.

PROFESSIONAL LEARNING ENVIRONMENT FOR EDUCATORS

Sometimes when we think about school improvement, we think of enhancing facilities; that is, the buildings and the grounds. Others may think about increasing the achievement of students. While we know that qualified teachers are needed to provide effective instruction, the professional environment for teachers is often overlooked. To provide a positive place where educators can continue to grow their own knowledge while affecting the students, higher-quality candidates who have the knowledge, skills, and training they need to be successful and effective must be identified (USDOE, 1983, 2008), especially in fields such as mathematics, science, foreign languages, and special education (USDOE, 1983).

Bandura's (1977) foundational research on self-efficacy, that is, a person's beliefs about self-ability to accomplish a task with competence or effectiveness in a specific domain, is essential to the formation of a positive climate among teachers. Creating school cultures and communities which generate open and honest conversations about school improvement and determine what is needed to make the enhancements more sustainable is essential. District leaders must create partnerships with school leaders and staff to develop deep understanding of necessary reform initiatives and to provide resources to promote those changes.

Collaborative Culture of Work

Teachers thrive in a collaborative culture of work. Throughout the literature, learning communities are emphasized as spaces for initiating school improvement. In a collaborative culture, daily learning is built into purposeful interaction among teachers, school leaders, and other school staff (Fullan, 2015). Fullan (2015) suggests that a collaborative culture centers on *time*: time to collaborate, time to reflect on teaching and learning, time to dedicate to professional learning, and time to plan individually and with others. Fullan (2014) recognizes the importance of the group and suggests that principals should spend more time cultivating the group to affect overall school success. Additionally, teachers who are interested in school leadership can be supported by school leaders by including them in opportunities and initiatives to improve schools.

Participation and Ownership

As schools conform to advances in technology, more effective teachers, who are fully involved in learning and presenting material to students in a way that is meaningful to the teachers and the students, are needed. Leaders must establish a culture that fosters and sustains transparency and trust among teachers, where teachers' opinions and suggestions are valued as educational professionals (Hipp & Huffman, 2010). As school structures change to operate with teams, teachers who relate their own teaching and learning to the overall success of their students seek additional means of collaboration to improve the schools. Without competition but rather knowing they are working as a team, teachers are more open to suggestions and critique of not only leaders but also their peers (Fairman & Mackenzie, 2015). Teachers should seek advice from mentor teachers and school leaders and take ownership of their own teaching and learning. School leaders must encourage teachers to have a growth mindset to positively affect the student population. Administrators and educators must be reflective partners who are open to redesigning curriculum and restructuring their schools for improvement.

Shared Leadership

School leaders must work with teachers to create an environment where everyone is valued for their unique contributions to the whole; the opportunity for shared leadership in schools is often a way to recognize what an individual can contribute to the school improvement efforts. Leithwood, Harris, and Hopkins (2008) identify influence, motivation, commitment, and the conditions of the school as basic tenets of successful school leadership. To build a culture of shared leadership, school leaders should form highly effective professional learning communities, encouraging teachers to use data collection and analysis in a process to identify strategies for improvement. In building a collaborative culture of work, shared leadership is the decision by teachers to share in learning and growth with and for each other, sometimes demonstrated in formal leadership roles (e.g., team leader, program director, curriculum coach) in the school and sometimes more informally (e.g., mentor to new teachers, head of field trips). Distributed leadership, in which roles and responsibilities are shared, differs slightly in that roles and responsibilities are more formally directed by the principal in the school.

Both shared and distributed leadership, however, are included in the overarching umbrella of collaborative leadership, which is most beneficial to school improvement efforts. When leadership is collaborative, teachers and school leaders are empowered by participating in decision-making and fostering shared accountability for student learning, giving ownership of that achievement to school leaders, teachers, and the students (Hallinger & Heck, 2010). Through collaborative leadership, student growth is positively impacted, evidenced in academic achievement in schools (Hallinger & Heck, 2010). Cultivating leadership qualities for emerging teachers to foster a sense of shared ownership improves schools.

Learning-Centered Leadership

To foster a holistic approach to school improvement, leadership should be centered on continual learning: student learning, teacher learning, and principal learning. In the time of high-stakes accountability, we must increase and refine professional development based on data collection and analysis to improve schools. While effective teaching is necessary, principals and superintendents also must have the "skills of persuasion, goal-setting, and developing community consensus" (USDOE, 2008, p. 7) through continual learning. Educators and legislators must be held accountable for providing school leadership necessary to achieve reforms and affect learning (USDOE, 1983).

Forging Academic Press

According to Murphy, Weil, Hallinger, and Mitman (1982), "Academic press is the degree to which environmental forces press for student achievement on a schoolwide basis" (p. 22). School leaders who apply academic press in a collaborative environment build successful teams that can provide direction for school improvement. Building capacity by strengthening skills, competencies, and abilities of those individuals within our schools provides a foundation for successful school reform. The Center on Education Policy (2012) suggests that leaders must build the capacity to reform and is necessary to change school climate to one of focus on positive academic press within the environment (Fullan, 2015).

Developing Supportive Culture

Gruenert (2005) provides a similar proposal when developing a supportive culture within schools, stating that "collaborative cultures seem to be the best setting for student achievement, thus affirming the literature on collaborative school cultures" (p. 50). The impact of professional learning communities and cultures of learning on school improvement is found across the literature, so school leaders must find a way to develop positive work relationships. Educators must constantly seek out, accept, and provide feedback, demonstrating a culture of support for one another in an effort to improve schools.

LEARNING-CENTERED LINKS TO SCHOOL COMMUNITY

To improve schools, partnerships with students, teachers, and staff within schools, states and local governments, and private organizations should be sought out by school leaders (Wise & Rothman, 2010). Furthermore, a connection to parents and families is essential in improving cultures and communities within schools (Klar, Huggins, Hammonds, & Buskey, 2016; Sigurðardóttir & Sigþórsson, 2016). By including parents, schools not only have support for students outside of school hours, but also increases the ability to tap into unchartered resources that are often hidden in the skills and aptitudes of those who entrust us with their children. By asserting a comprehensive model of leadership school partnership, schools must examine opportunities of the external environment as well as internal organizational processes (Hallinger & Heck, 2010).

MONITORING OF PROGRESS AND PERFORMANCE ACCOUNTABILITY

School leaders must monitor progress within the school, focusing on formative and summative data as well as anecdotal data, to make decisions. Typically, when we think of monitoring progress, we think of academic achievement; however, school leaders are responsible for much more. In school improvement efforts, school leaders must assess success or failure as process is unfolding, adjusting procedures as necessary while allowing enough time to gather adequate data to make decisions.

Performance-Based Goals

Whether the subject is academic achievement or any other area of improvement, leaders must set high standards with measurable goals (Cross, 2015). Academic goals must be focused on student improvement and can be assessed through achievement tests, which measure current student performance, or aptitude tests, which predict future performance. Schools must implement standards-based curriculum with clear, grade-specific requirements (USDOE, 2008) and, based on federal mandates, administer standardized tests at major transition points in education. In addition to standardized tests, school leaders must find a way to allow students with varying needs the opportunity for growth.

Systematic Use of Data

To monitor improvement, school leaders must employ transparent use of student data to drive decision making and to improve instruction (DuFour & Mattos, 2013). NCLB held schools accountable for student achievement, requiring documentation of achievement and issuing penalties for schools that did not make adequate yearly progress (Forte, 2010; Johnson, 2013; Wise & Rothman, 2010). Just as schools examine achievement data as a measure of student learning, student data also are used for evaluating teachers, requiring teachers to have a positive impact on students to continue in the profession. Advances in technology allow this data to be more readily available than in the past and thus, can be used for evaluative purposes; however, data are not limited to state standardized tests but also may include anecdotal teacher data. While data are more accessible, consideration must be given to accountability systems in place and whether there is adequate knowledge to use data garnered from such systems (Superfine, 2005).

Shared Accountability

Evaluating performance and embedding measures of accountability are required as part of the early education legislation and have continued as components of the more recent mandates (Mills, 2008). Accountability, however, sometimes seems to have a tongue-in-cheek effect: if teachers are held accountable for student learning, then students must be accountable for their own achievement, showing adequate performance to be promoted from one grade to another or be placed in a lower level educational track (Superfine, 2005). School leaders must find a way to share accountability for student achievement between all stakeholders and work with each to promote school improvement.

CHANGING ROLE OF SCHOOL LEADERS

The principal's role is complex with both leadership and management responsibilities that evolve as state and federal mandates shift thinking about the educational processes (Seashore, 2009). This role has changed dramatically through the years. In past decades, principals were viewed as the figure head of the school, the school planners, and problem solvers. Principals' base of influence then moved to one of "professional expertise and moral imperative rather than line authority" (Murphy, 2015, p. 17). Leaders must be actors, negotiating the political arena and playing peacemaker between legislators, school districts, teachers, and other stakeholders. In a time of educational transformation, principals became change agents who could navigate the waters of educational policy, accountability, and achievement (Seashore, 2009). Most recently, school leaders have taken on the role of instructional leaders as well as managers (USDOE, 2008).

The principal is at the heart of learning: requiring learning, leading learning, and modeling learning. Providing opportunities for shared leadership within schools involves teachers, those at the very heart of the educational body, to affect student learning and development. School leadership must take into account the culture of the school, including students, teachers, leaders, and other stakeholders, realizing that those affecting school improvement want to contribute and can be trusted to do so; the role of the school leader in developing culture is to model a process of learning and achievement (Seashore, 2009).

While focusing on school improvement, how schools develop in compliance with reform mandates while continuing to focus on student growth should be a focus. Rapidly increasing demands of global economy with an education system that is not keeping up with demands is problematic. In an effort to meet challenges associated with school improvement, principals must change their leadership structure by cultivating leadership within the school. In their research, Leithwood, Louis, Anderson, and Wahlstrom (2004) highlight three elements for high quality leaders who impact student performance: set directions and expectations, use data to analyze outcomes; develop people by providing professional learning opportunities and supportive resources to reach the intended goals; and create a working organization that enhances high quality teaching and learning with the ultimate goal of student success.

CONCLUSION

A Nation at Risk identified the United States as "a nation informed, a nation accountable, and a nation that recognizes there is much work to be done" (USDOE, 2008, p. 1). While total per-pupil spending has increased dramatically, US students are still not performing on the same level as international counterparts (USDOE, 2008). Federal accountability mandates have not provided funding to make necessary improvements, so school leaders are left to develop innovative ways to assure quality teaching, affect student achievement, evaluate schools, and ensure stakeholder involvement (Adelman & Taylor, 2011; Anderson, 2002; Darling-Hammond, 2010; Desimone, 2002; Forte, 2010; Johnson, 2013; Lee & Luykx, 2005).

The US has widespread challenges in education and cannot allow these challenges to go unaddressed (Wise & Rothman, 2010). From decades of educational research and reform, we know more about what works and what investments we must make to improve our schools. For children to be effective in a global economy, we must invest in adolescent literacy. School leaders should hire professionals who can support students' attainment of basic skills, alignment of curriculum to state tests, and short term strategies to boost achievement scores (Au & Valencia, 2010). We must equip our students with higher ordering thinking, comprehension, critical thinking, reasoning, and problem solving strategies to help them succeed.

As school leaders, we must find creative ways to fund school reform to fully implement school improvement strategies. We must provide equitable conditions in schools and classrooms to ensure all students can learn and all teachers can teach (Au & Valencia, 2010). We must shift our focus from accountability to progress with a core mission of helping all students achieve. These must be long-term changes that promote a culture of teacher and student engagement with teachers and administrators who are reflective practitioners with a consistent focus on school improvement.

REFERENCES

Adelman, H., & Taylor, L. (2011). Turning around, transforming, and continuously improving schools: Policy proposals are still based on two- rather than a three-component blueprint. *The International Journal on School Disaffection, 8*(1), 22–34.

Anderson, R. D. (2002). Reforming science teaching: What research says about inquiry. *Journal of Science Teacher Education, 13*(1), 1–12.

Au, K. H., & Valencia, S. W. (2010). Fulfilling the potential of standards-based education: Promising policy principles. *Language Arts, 87*(5), 373–380.

Bandura, A. (1977). Self-efficacy: Toward a unifying theory of behavioral change. *Psychological Review, 84*(2), 191.

Center on Education Policy. (2012). *Changing the school climate is the first step to reform in many schools with federal improvement grants.* Washington, DC: McMurrer.

Coleman, J. S. (1966). *Equality of educational opportunity.* Washington, DC: United States Office of Education.

Cross, C. T. (2015). The shaping of federal education policy over time. *The Progress of Education Reform, 16*(2), 1–6.

Darling-Hammond, L. (2010). *The flat world and education: How America's commitment to equity will determine our future.* New York, NY: Teachers College Press.

Desimone, L. (2002). How can comprehensive school reform models be successfully implemented? *Review of Educational Research, 72*(3), 433–479.

DuFour, R., & Mattos, M. (2013). How do principals really improve schools? *Educational Leadership, 70*(7), 34–40.

Elementary and Secondary Education Act of 1965, PL 89–10, 79 Stat. 27 (1965).

Fairman, J. C., & Mackenzie, S. V. (2015). How teacher leaders influence others and understand their leadership. *International Journal of Leadership in Education, 18*(1), 61–87. https://doi.org/10.1080/13603124.2014.904002

Forte, E. (2010). Examining the assumptions underlying the NCLB federal accountability policy on school improvement. *Educational Psychologist, 45*(2), 76–88.

Fullan, M. (2014). *The principal: Three keys to maximizing impact.* San Francisco, CA: Josey Bass.

Fullan, M. (2015). *The new meaning of educational change.* New York, NY: Teachers College Press.

Gruenert, S. (2005). Correlations of collaborative school cultures with student achievement. *NASSP Bulletin, 89*(645), 43–55. https://doi.org/10.1177/019263650508964504

Hallinger, P., & Heck, R. H. (2010). Leadership for learning: Does collaborative leadership make a difference in school improvement? *Educational Management Administration and Leadership, 38*(6), 654–678. https://doi.org/10.1177/1741143210379060

Hipp, K. K., & Huffman, J. B. (2010). *Demystifying professional learning communities: Leadership at its best.* New York, NY: Rowman & Littlefield Education.

Jencks, C., & Brown, M. (1975). The effects of desegregation on student achievement: Some new evidence from the equality of educational opportunity survey. *Sociology of Education, 48*(1), 126–140.

Johnson, C. C. (2013). Educational turbulence: The influence of macro and micro-policy on science education reform. *Journal of Science Teacher Education, 24*, 693–715.

Klar, H. W., Huggins, K. S., Hammonds, H. L., & Buskey, F. C. (2016). Fostering the capacity for distributed leadership: A post-heroic approach to leading school improvement. *International Journal of Leadership in Education, 19*(2), 111–137. https://doi.org/10.1080/13603124.2015.1005028

Lee, L., & Luykx, A. (2005). Dilemmas in scaling up innovations in elementary science instruction with nonmainstream students. *Science Education, 9*(3), 371–383.

Leithwood, K., Harris, A., & Hopkins, D. (2008). Seven strong claims about successful school leadership. *School Leadership and Management, 28*(1), 27–42. https://doi.org/10.1080/13632430701800060

Leithwood, K., Louis, K. S., Anderson, G., & Wahlstrom, K. (2004). *How leadership influences student learning: A review of research for the learning from leadership project.* New York, NY: The Wallace Foundation.

Mills, J. (2008). A legislative overview of No Child Left Behind. *New Directions for Higher Education, 117*, 9–20. https://doi.org/10.1002/ev

Murphy, J. (2013). The architecture of school improvement. *Journal of Educational Administration, 51*(3), 252–263.

Murphy, J. (2015, November). Forces shaping schooling and school leadership. *Journal of School Leadership, 25*, 1056–1087.

Murphy, J. F., Weil, M., Hallinger, P., & Mitman, A. (1982). Academic press: Translating high expectations into school policies and classroom practices. *Educational Leadership, 40*(3), 2226.

Seashore, K. R. (2009). Leadership and change in schools: Personal reflections over the last 30 years. *Journal of Educational Change, 10*, 129–140.

Sigurðardóttir, S. M., & Sigþórsson, R. (2016). The fusion of school improvement and leadership capacity in an elementary school. *Educational Management Administration and Leadership, 44*(4), 599–616. https://doi.org/10.1177/1741143214559230

Superfine, B. M. (2005). The politics of accountability: The rise and fall of Goals 2000. *American Journal of Education, 112*(1), 10–43.

United States Department of Education. (1983). *A Nation at Risk: The imperative for educational reform: A report to the Nation and the Secretary of Education, United States Department of Education.* Washington, DC: Author:

United States Department of Education. (2008). *A nation accountable: Twenty-five years after A Nation at Risk.* Retrieved from https://www2.ed.gov/rschstat/research/pubs/accountable/accountable.pdf

Wise, B., & Rothman, R. (2010). A greater society: The transformation of the federal role in education. *New Directions for Youth Development, 127*, 123–131. doi: 10.1002/yd.368

ABOUT THE AUTHORS

Jami Royal Berry is a clinical assistant professor in the Educational Administration and Policy Program at the University of Georgia and a co-director of the UCEA Center for the International Study of Educational Leadership. Berry has served as a facilitator for the Educational Development Center, as a consultant for the Educational Testing Service, as the president of the Georgia Educational Leadership Faculty Association, as a member of multiple Georgia Professional Standards Commission task forces, and as a guest speaker for organizations including the University Council for Educational Administration, the Georgia Association of Secondary School Principals, the Georgia School Boards Association, and the Georgia Professional Standards Commission. Berry's research interests include leadership in high needs schools, leadership certification, the performance-based leadership model, and the supervisor's role in leadership internships, and she has presented and written on these topics nationally and internationally. She has developed numerous educational leadership programs and served as a dissertation chairperson or committee member for over twenty doctoral students. Her graduates include local school leaders, system level leaders, and superintendents throughout Georgia and the United States. Prior to her university service, she was a music teacher and elementary school administrator. She remains active in K–12 education through volunteering in schools and serving as a board member for several local education organizations.

Cherie Barnett Gaines began her career in 2001 as a middle school teacher of science, reading, and English. After earning her doctoral degree from The University of Tennessee, Knoxville, in Education with a concentration in Educational Administration and Supervision, she began work in higher education at Lincoln Memorial University (LMU), Knoxville, Tennessee, where she worked in Initial Teacher Licensure programs. While at LMU, Dr. Gaines has served as Director of Clinical Experiences for the School of Education, focusing on accreditation. Currently, Dr. Gaines is an Assistant Professor of Education in the doctoral program for Education at LMU. Cherie's research interests include rural schools, teacher leadership, school climate, social justice, middle school education, and leadership preparation. As a member of the American Educational Research Association's Leadership for School Improvement Special Interest Group, she focuses her research on school improvement in those research areas. Dr. Gaines has presented research at conference meetings such as American Educational Research Association, Mid-South Educational Research Association, and British Educational Leadership, Management & Administration Society, and her work can be found in journals such as *NASSP Bulletin* and in several published books.

Julia Kirk has served as a business teacher in grades 5–12, a curriculum and technology integration facilitator, an instructional coach, and a building level administrator at both the elementary and middle school level in two school districts in East Tennessee. Additionally, Dr. Kirk has served as a Regional Data Analyst and Executive Director of the Center of Regional Excellence in the First TN district of the state of Tennessee. Through all of these roles in the K–12 systems in East Tennessee, Dr. Kirk focused on school improvement through a balanced assessment system, data analysis, professional learning communities, and response to instruction and intervention. Dr. Kirk has served as both an adjunct and Assistant Professor at Lincoln Memorial University. She teaches courses in the Instructional Leadership and Curriculum and Instruction concentration. Dr. Kirk earned her Doctor of Philosophy in Educational Psychology and Research with a major in Adult Education, a cognate in Instructional Technology, and a certification in Educational Administration from the University of Tennessee, Knoxville in 2012. Dr. Kirk also holds a Masters in Business Education from Middle Tennessee State University and a Bachelors in Accounting from the University of Tennessee, Knoxville.

Nate Koerber is a Graduate Teaching Assistant at the University of Tennessee and a first-year doctoral student studying Education Leadership and Policy. His research interests include educational law, social justice leadership, collaborative leadership, and educating and empowering students with diverse language backgrounds.

David J. Lomascolo is a Policy Analyst at Chapin Hall at the University of Chicago. Dr. Lomascolo's work focuses on the use of organizational assessment, applying principles from safety science to inform child welfare policy and practice improvement initiatives. In addition to organizational assessment, Dr. Lomascolo's areas of expertise include policy research, professional development and workforce readiness assessments, and survey design and implementation. In his current role, Dr. Lomascolo works closely with state governments across the country, focusing on ways to enhance training, professional development, and safety culture for workers in child welfare organizations. David holds a Ph.D. in Education with a concentration in Leadership Studies from the University of Tennessee, where he was an Orin Graff Scholar, a Master of Science in Education from The College of Saint Rose and a Bachelor of Arts in History from Siena College.

James A. Martinez currently serves as an Assistant Professor in the Department of Educational Leadership and Policy Studies at the University of Tennessee, Knoxville. Dr. Martinez's research focuses on interventions to support early career teachers / administrators who serve marginalized students. He is the National Co-Leader of the Secondary Teacher Retention in Diverse Educational Settings (STRIDES) Research Action Cluster. After working for Rockwell International as a mechanical engineer on the Space Shuttle, Dr. Martinez served as a classroom teacher and school administrator for seventeen years. He and his wife, Elizabeth, live in Knoxville, Tennessee, and enjoy outdoor adventures and local theater performances with their two adult children and 9 year-old Labrador retriever.

Dianne F. Olivier, Professor in Educational Foundations and Leadership at the University of Louisiana at Lafayette, serves as Coordinator of the Doctoral Program and holds the Joan D. and Alexander S. Haig/BORSF Endowed Professorship in Education. Dr. Olivier received the University Research Excellence Award, 2014–2016, as well as the University Outstanding Doctoral Mentor Award for 2014–2016 and 2013–2014, having served as Chair for over 50 doctoral dissertations. Dr. Olivier's research focuses on educational leadership, professional learning communities, school culture, and teacher self- and collective efficacy. She has developed several assessments and has authored/coauthored book chapters and articles relating to her research interests. Her PLC research has transitioned from the domestic national level to a global perspective as a member of a Global PLC Network and she has been invited to conduct international presentations in Australia, Canada, Hong Kong, Indonesia, Singapore, Taiwan, and China. Prior to the university level, Dr. Olivier served thirty-four years in public education with twenty-six of those years as a district administrator. She uses her former

K–12 administrative experiences to work throughout the U.S. with principals, central office personnel, and teacher leaders in her role as an educational consultant with the Learning-Centered Leadership Program for the Southern Regional Education Board.

Margaret M. Ritchie is a Clinical Instructor and doctoral student in the Educational Leadership and Policy Studies Department at The University of Tennessee, Knoxville, USA, and coordinates the VOLS Online Leadership Preparation Program. Her research interests include leadership succession and transition.

www.ingramcontent.com/pod-product-compliance
Lightning Source LLC
Chambersburg PA
CBHW070624300426
44113CB00010B/1645